Volume 4: Fulfilling a Destiny

Decisions Decisions: Getting Answers to Life's Challenges   Large Print Edition

Haneefa Mateen

Copyright © 2023 by Haneefa Mateen

All rights reserved.

ISBN 978-1-73772-19-7-0

No portion of this book may be reproduced in any form without written permission from the publisher or author, except as permitted by U.S. copyright law.

Acknowledgment is gratefully given to the authors of the book, Physicians of the Heart: A Sufi View of the Ninety-Nine Names of Allah, for granting permission to use their list and explanations of the ninety-nine names of Allah, in Chapter 18 in this book. Copyright © 2011 by Wali Ali Meyer, Bilal Hyde, Faisal Muqaddam, Shabda Khan. Sufi Ruhaniat International.

Disclaimer: The author of this book, Decisions, Decisions' stories, experiences and opinions are from author's perspective and are not intended as medical advice or the use of any techniques as a form of treatment for physical, medical, psychiatric, mental health problems either directly or indirectly. The intent of the author is only to share experiences in a general nature in her quest for emotional and spiritual wellbeing. In the event that you use any of the information in this book for yourself, which is your constitutional right, the author and publisher

COPYRIGHT

assumes no responsibility or liability whatsoever for readers or purchasers of this book.

Decisions, Decisions is a non-fiction story, however some names, locations, and other identifying information were changed to protect privacy of individuals.

Book Cover art: Haneefa Mateen

Contents

Introduction	1
Chapter 1: Destiny Progress	9
Chapter 2: Rethinking Education	28
Chapter 3: A Difficult to Understand Spiritual Reading:	40
Chapter 4: Oshun's Blessings	54
Chapter 5: Sekert (Oya's) Influences on My Destiny	65
Chapter 6: Healing the Past	77

Chapter 7: The Beautiful Ninety-Nine Names of Allah: Wazifa Card Set	84
Chapter 8: Facing Death and Loss	118
Chapter 9: A Friend Responds Through a Medium Message	130
Chapter 10: Ochosi Revisited	152
Chapter 11: Getting Rid of Clutter	176
Chapter 12: Spiritual Transformation	187
Chapter 13: Career Path	196
Chapter 14: Another Tough Assignment	213

Chapter 15: Applying Accumulated Wisdom to How I Provide Psychotherapy	224
Chapter 16: Work on What Has Been Spoiled	233
Conclusion	240
Books and Articles	244
Author's Bio	253

Introduction

If you lose sleep because you're worried that you still don't know your life purpose, natural talents and career yet, there's hope. Hopefully, you are inspired to learn more about your own life purpose, as you follow along my journey with some of the tools and strategies I use to make major decisions, and to learn about myself and my life purpose. Keep in mind, I'd lived half of my life before I was introduced to these indigenous or ancient concepts. In amazement, while learning different cultures' divination and then looked back on my past, what I saw was very accurate. And you will too.

I was first introduced to the concept of oracle cards and divination through an African-centered church, the Ausar Auset Society Church in 1991. They had weekly classes where I learned about ancient African history, philosophy, and cosmology's different ways of viewing the world. They taught us about improving our health, because poor health affects our ability to manage our own emotions and behavior. This included spiritual health as we wonder, what's the reason and purpose for living? Why bother to get up in the morning day after day? There's got to be more to life than this? Why does this keep happening to me?

Why do I feel so lonely and empty? Why did I keep choosing the same type of relationships, the same dudes?

In these Ausar Auset Society Church classes, I began to get answers to these life challenges, though I didn't understand much in the beginning, I just followed along. Attendees were instructed to first get a destiny reading also known as an incarnation objective from a priest. A "reading" is a spiritual guidance consultation. The reason for a destiny reading is to learn your purpose for having been born on Earth at this time, and what lessons you are to learn. Later, we learned how to do our own spiritual readings using oracle cards or coins.

These destiny and other spiritual readings are not meant for fortune-telling. Divination is to help you grow emotionally, mentally, heal physically, build a strong spiritual character with responsibility to community, therefore having success with true abundance in all areas of your life. After doing the initial destiny readings, then you can ask about your destiny or life lessons at more frequent intervals such as daily or monthly. Later, you can inquire about specific situations or projects that you are in, or you wish to be involved in. But all readings are to be referred back to your destiny reading. In other words, ask yourself, "How does what I want to do, and the current spiritual reading help me to fulfill my destiny?"

Shekum ur Shekum, the founder and leader of the Ausar Auset Society

Church a Pan-African spirituality church, commented in one of his classes that one day someone should write a book showing how their own destiny and spiritual readings and understanding evolved. I was surprised when he mentioned this idea, because he previously taught that what is in each individual's journal notebook is private. It was emphasized that no one sneak and read anyone else's notebook without permission. However, since I am in my later years of life, and knew several people who came to Ausar Auset Society Church who told me they did not understand and therefore didn't benefit from the teachings or spiritual practices, I've decided to share some of mine. I greatly benefited from Ausar Auset Society Church and it was a springboard for the rest of my life.

This book is a cumulation of 30 years of studying and using various different cultures' divination methods.

With time, I began to understand the difference between being spiritual and being religious. Religion is the beliefs, scriptures, practices, rules and rituals often taught to us by communities, that we do together with other people, often at a place of worship. Religions and holy scriptures tend to threaten human beings with damnation and going to hell for our transgressions, yet don't tell or show us how to stay out of hell. Just, "don't do this or don't do that" with contradictory messages of "we were born in sin," "confess and you'll be forgiven," and don't let the devil temp you." To be honest, I've tried and tried to understand the Bible and the Quran initially translated in old English, with stories I can't relate to in our current days and times. Religious leaders are no help as they argue over the meanings.

Spirituality is the inner peace, calm, satisfaction, sense of purpose for living, faith, and connection to self and the universe. Of course, like other people, I use both religion and spirituality as I learned prayers and rituals from different religions and cultures. The use of oracles and other forms of divination can show each of us, as well as our families and communities how to stay out of unnecessary hell in both this life (and the next).

Hopefully this book, Volume 4: Fulfilling a Destiny, introduces you to different perspectives as my personal stories bring understanding of how ancient and now popularized practices for making decisions — when used properly — brings improved quality of life, inner peace, satisfaction, and sense of purpose. And is inspirational to you on your own life's journey.

By the end of this book, hopefully we will have both gained wisdom about the meaning of a long life.

Chapter 1: Destiny Progress

After saying a prayer asking for guidance in 1991, the first question I asked was about my destiny. I shuffled and spread the Metu Neter oracle deck, closed my eyes and pulled the Het-Heru Hetep card. From the Ausar Auset Church classes and books, I learned that with a Het-Heru destiny, that throughout my life I should strive to be joyful, to experience pleasure in healthy balanced ways, be sociable, harmonious with others and nature, and appreciate the beauty in all. Further, I'm to be aware of how I use my imagination in my thoughts and daydreaming fantasies as these could come true in life. Strong inner joy and pleasure raises the life-force which will inspire and motivate me towards passionately fulfilling my goals. Best to decrease tendencies to be timid, seeking too much pleasure, wanting to feel good all the time by daydreaming or using intoxicating drugs, alcohol, sex and other addictions to avoid unpleasant tasks and responsibilities. Careers to consider are all kinds of artists: dancers, musicians, singers, writers, entertainers, make-up artists, fashion designers, interior decorators, drawers, painters, graphic designers, and animators. Het Heru is also known as Osun in the Yoruba traditions.

At 66 years old, let us together see how far I have come in fulfilling my destiny. Hopefully, you have already read Volume 1, Volume 2 and Volume 3 of this book series, <u>Decisions Decisions</u>, that has stories of my younger years and how I got to where I am now.

You can help me judge my progress as an outsider looking in. Could be near the end of my incarceration as my parents lived to their early 60's and 70's, or I could be halfway since my grandmother lived to be 106-years-old. This timeframe is of course is in terms of a Western idea of a chronological lifetime. Some people are done with their true destinies at much younger ages. From what you've read of my divined destiny goals, let's review how have I done.

Het Heru Hetep (Oshun)

Relationships

Well . . .while the creative aspects of Het Heru are flourishing . . . I've probably failed in the romantic relationship love area of my life. Or at least need to hurry up and put my concentration in that direction.

Sex? Sometimes behind closed eyes, recently, I imagined what it would be like to have someone lying beside me holding me close. What if television dramas and movies were true about heterosexual intercourse being exciting, painless, enjoyable, nurturing, caring, beneficial and healing? Get so hot down there that you gotta have it right then and there. He wants you and you want him. Then my mind slides down memory lane. He's bigger, stronger, dominating. He takes up most of the bed. He has to have the television on loud all night, with the windows open in the wintertime. Whatever he's seen and expects, has to be performed on him regardless of what I may want? Or that he's been with someone else and may or may not be honest enough to say, "Honey, you need to go get checked at the Board of Health."

"What for? I feel fine. I had my annual physical already."

Too young to understand. Now I'm older. Perhaps older and wiser. But who cares about wiser?

The song, "I want to thank you" by Alicia Meyers, came into my head recently upon awakening. I'm hoping it is a sign that my desire for a companion is answered. I liked this song decades ago, but at that time I turned it into a praise song to God. Now I'm hoping that the lyrics, "I want to thank you, heavenly Father for shining your light on me. You sent me someone who really loves me and not just my body. It took a long time for it to happen. I prayed a long time for it to happen, but I knew those nights I prayed, that you would send me someone who is real and not someone for play" will come true for me. Appreciated for who we are. Not just our bodies or what our bodies can do for someone else.

I'm hoping that the COVID pandemic crisis has taught us all too well that people are precious. Since being shut in, I've craved and prayed for someone, or that a group of people comes into my life, who have also been doing their emotional growth, maturing, now ready to have someone else along for the journey, able to appreciate, respect and value themselves and others.

A year ago, I kept hearing the song lyric, "I am getting married in the morning" so often that it was annoying! No one has showed up yet, at least that I've recognized. Maybe they tried, and I wasn't paying attention. A companion, a true companion is what my heart desires. Marriage is the furthest from my mind, I've been there and done that twice. Sex is something I don't have to have. I had sex in my marriages only because society taught me that that's what I was supposed to do. So I'm not sure what the message means. Perhaps, my heart needs to open and trust more. And I could read more romance novels instead of only nonfiction books!

In regards to I Ching hexagrams 8 and 45 guidance for moving to Chicago, it took time, fifteen long years of living here for me to find and gather together with people of like mind, mostly after my having to heal first, then being introduced to the Church of the Spirit, and later becoming a psychologist.

Beauty

Winter solstice 2021 <u>Sacred Path Card Workbook</u> spiritual guidance reading asked the question, "Have you been neglecting your appearance?" Yes.

Well. . .well…does being at home in my jogging suit or pajamas during the

COVID pandemic shutdown give me an excuse? I was getting dressed everyday wearing a different color top and sometimes different color trousers, but then that meant my laundry was piling up. My helper was only coming once a month. After getting pain in my abdominal hernia from lifting, I decided not to be the superwoman, to instead compromise, and be more like everybody else.

A monumental question is, "Whose idea of beauty?" By extension, how should my appearance be? What do I do with comments like, "I like it when you let your hair down." "You have beautiful white hair. You should show it more often?"

I could possibly think about doing that. But again, isn't my hair beautiful no matter what hairstyle? Why do I only get compliments during the winter when my hair naturally straightens out?

At my age, my hair is too thin to style it like I used to. With a receding hairline, you can't see much of my hair on Zoom unless I sit sideways, which I do occasionally. It is really strange though, that I get these comments when I am the only dark complexion person in the room. Often don't compliment the other women's (or men's) hair, so why not comment on my skin instead of my almost nonexistent hair? Ah ha, duh because I'm also the only one with naturally gray hair!

Recently, I saw a "Red Table Talk" video on the increasing popularity of African American women shaving their hair bald. Jada Pinkett Smith and her daughter Willow, and the rest of the women are absolutely beautiful! Having a bald head or a low-cut brings out our natural facial features. They talked about feeling free.

Freedom. I know some of that freedom of just being able to shower, grease up, and go. In the past, I used to cut my hair every 10 years, usually because I'd grown tired of having a full head of hair down to my shoulders. It was so thick it took 12 hours to dry naturally. I couldn't tolerate the hot heat of a dryer, so I combed and braided my hair immediately after shampooing it and let it dry. Therefore, I only washed my hair once a week. The rest of the days, I let it down if I chose to, and then braided it in small braids before bed at night. That was a lot of work.

Many people don't know or think about how much damage perms and weaves do to African American hair and scalp. Neither did I know weaves did long term damage, until I saw the "Red Table Talk" video. African American women are shaving their hair because harsh hair treatments are causing alopecia bald spots where the hair doesn't grow back. India Arie sang about women without hair after chemotherapy in her hit single, "I Am Not My Hair" in 2006. The main lyric words are, "I am not my hair, I am not my skin. I am the soul that lives within." I'm really, really, really wishing that we could accept each other for the natural beauty we all have inside and out.

When I was younger, I dreamed of designing and styling my hair in big bold ways similar to the models' hairstyles on the fashion show runways. It's wonderful that my hair is now growing down my back, since I don't comb it everyday like I used to do, when I went out to the university or to work. Gray hair is brittle, sheds, and breaks off easier, so I try not to stress my hair too much. I will be learning new ways to style my hair, especially since I can't find gray bobby pins to match my hair color. Paying $12 for a small package of thirty gray hair pins that still showed in my hair was ridiculous, but I had given in to a friend's teasing. However, now that I am aware of my nearing the end of my destiny, I want to be able to check that dream goal off of my bucket list. So while other people are going bald, I am letting my hair grow longer.

Recently, people male, female, old and young approach me and tell me how beautiful my silver-gray hair is, and how pretty, smooth, young and glowing my face looks. They ask me, "What do you use? Other than being calmer, with less worries, and therefore less wrinkles the only change has been hopefully a deeper sleep and natural vitamins with more iron. Just water on my face folks, same as I've done since I was a teenager.

Creativity: The Artist

So far with what I've written and reviewed of my life, there is a lot of warrior and counseling energy but not much about creativity. So how has creativity been at my core, my strength that keeps me going?

Probably I would not be me if I wasn't doing some kind of art. Even during times when I've felt too busy and overwhelmed to do art, such as in graduate school, someone will inevitably ask me to do an art project or will need a problem solved. Yet somehow, I find the time. Knitted baby clothes for my adopted daughter's firstborn. Mittens for children and people who were homeless. Custom make African American dolls because since my childhood, there are still very few dolls that look like us. Quickly learned how to quilt after I got tired of being cold at night with much too short, acrylic fake fleece blankets. Out of necessity with a sense of urgency,

I wrote books. Creatively cook with whatever I have or can find at the farmers' market because of the COVID pandemic high cost of food. The list goes on.

Why make everyone one else rich but us, if we can make it ourselves? I've felt that way since I was a teenager. Buying jeans with someone else's initials or logo, and calling them designer jeans didn't make sense to me. Am I not a designer too? I embroidered butterflies on the back pockets. Also sewed my own jeans to fit my long torso and crotch with a small but bigger African American butt than store bought jeans. Otherwise to sit in women's jeans for more than an hour was painful torture.

I'm still the Amateur archetype in that I enjoy making art, but only sold a few of my creations, some are stashed away or I give my art away or sell it at low prices. My creativity, however, had taken the place of socializing with my family, friends, and community. So has years of university education. I heard of perpetual students, but I had not intended to become one! When I was younger, I thought college was stupid because the money that people spend on college is a down payment or the entire price for buying a house or financing a business. My conscience really bothered me while I was in the doctoral program. Scholarships, and student loans with stipends each semester were given freely without considering one's credit history. Yet, African Americans aren't given loans for businesses and for owning homes in their communities. I felt guilty for having this privilege just because I could excel in school.

Chapter 2: Rethinking Education

North American feminists say they are concerned about how we can help the women in Afghanistan. The Taliban are reported to be taking away education and jobs from girls and women. But have we considered what is education? How many years should education be? How much of the education that we have, do we actually use? How does the education in the United States help us survive? Are we taught survival skills in school? When starving can we eat the textbooks that we bought? Or the computers and smart phones that we can't really afford?

Water is a primary necessity, more essential than education. But why is it the women's responsibility to haul heavy water? How did this come to be? Boys and men go to school and then to work, usually to do migrant work in near by or foreign countries. Education for only a chosen few, and of these, only a few are hired. How did it come to be that we think that working in someone else's factory sweat shop, office, store, home, or school is required for survival? Previously, everyone including men would simply walk to the stream, river, or gather snow for their own drink of water. No one owned the land. Anyone could eat freely of the wild fruits and vegetables. But colonizers came in and took the land from the people. With modern day slaveowners or rebel gangs forcing people to grow inedible crops like cotton, poppies for opium, coca for cocaine, etc., then too much edible crops are also exported to other countries for them to get rich and fat, while your own family barely eats and is paid subsistence wages, therefore you are forced to continue working in the fields to survive. Sharecropping. Your soil ruined, eroded, dried and cracked from excessive commercial farming. Then the rain stops as there is no water going up to come down as rain, and rivers and lakes are redirected for hydroelectric power for the rich people and the cities. So called "developed countries" make sure other countries stay poor.

What happens to relationships and families when our focus is predominantly on education and careers? When the child is "smarter" than the parents, but doesn't know own culture? Or how to survive. Education and careers separate families and communities, as children and the breadwinner go off to faraway places to get the best that's offered. "Brain drain" is when the young educated away to other countries or other areas for employment, depriving their own communities of the experts and professionals that their parents sacrificed and risked investment in. Too often, young adults don't return to live in their home communities.

I haven't returned to my home community after going away to college the first time, as I unexpectedly continued on to graduate school. Honestly, I didn't know what a master's degree was. I didn't know what a PhD was. I knew about a master's in nursing. That was about it. In order to be a nurse practitioner you have to have a master's degree, and now there are nurses with PhD's. I hadn't planned to go onto a doctorate degree. It just happened. And of course, with the amount of assignments for two years at the master's level, I wasn't thinking about more school.

But I was online one day and typed in Argosy University because I had brochures from when I applied there in 1998 a little after I came back from

Zimbabwe. I looked over the website and needed more information, but instead the website didn't give it to me. A chat box came up. So I typed in my phone number, and was startled by my home phone ringing as soon as I put in the last number. I ended up talking to one of the admission's staff. She was a great salesperson and told me I only had two weeks to get all of my application materials in. This meant rushing to order and pick up my transcripts.

Of course, yes, I did an I Ching reading first. This reading is similar to when I inquired about going to the Argosy University in 1998 and got Hexagram 42 Increase (Maat) (lines 1 and 6) into hexagram 8 Union. Amen Hetep. It's furthers one to do something great and to sacrifice your own life to help others. Must work on one's own flaws first by getting spiritual help. By living a spiritual life, you will receive abundance, and the strength and energy to carry out one's new increased responsibilities. Warned that if you don't share with others, then you may incur more crises and disasters in your life.

From 1999, I was given time, almost 10 years — of hexagram 33 Retreat from employment — to work on my flaws, heal my own traumas, and gain confidence before I could counsel others. After this personal growth, was I now ready to attend Argosy University?

I asked again in 2010 and received Hexagram 19 Approach that describes an idealistic situation favorable in the beginning with people coming together, those in a higher position helping people in the lower positions. However, this is time limited as I found out the hard way. After the first year there was very little support from the administrators of the university. Hexagram 19 advised it was best that I reach out for help but it is also important to find the right person. I needed this encouragement because I wasn't good at asking for help, but after that first year of graduate school I was forced to ask for help. Line 6 of hexagram 19 is guidance about coming into the world with a weakened body and the need to heal the body before can go out in the world to work. Hexagram 19 is the complement of Hexagram 33 Retreat. There is return after retreating and now was the time to return.

Metu Neter: Ausar tem maat/ Amen tu maat is about the need for me being unified and calm within, and with others. Taking neither gain nor loss to heart. This aspiration was sorely tested.

While I was in Philadelphia visiting my family at my grandmother's house, I had my admission's interview over the phone. Two hours later they told me I was accepted, and I could start either in January or in the fall. I just took these synchronous events as a sign from heaven.

The other reason I continued on to the clinical psychology doctoral program was because although everyone in the master's level counseling program had the same required counseling courses, the rehabilitation counseling classes was mostly about how to help people get jobs. For those who had intellectual disabilities and were in special education classes in high schools, as they became adults, we helped them transition to the workshops and set them up with job coaches. This had little to do with therapeutic counseling. Ever since 1990, when I first went to therapy myself, I have wanted to help people who had experienced trauma to heal.

What put the nail in the coffin, as far as me being a rehabilitation counselor was that my vocational counselor started sending me email after email with want ads for working at McDonald's and Burger King. Seems there is some kind of rule that if you get rehabilitation services then you need to at least work a job for 90 days before the Department of Human Services Office of Rehabilitation Services can get paid. So she didn't care where I worked. I would never do that to a client who uses a wheelchair! Like could you see me flipping burgers in a wheelchair? Where would I ever fit in a McDonald's kitchen? Now that I think about it, I'd be in the way, while they are running back-and-forth with the french fries and burgers. Plus that, I had graduated with a master's degree. That's an insult on top of insult. I know there are plenty of people who have graduated from college who are flipping hamburgers because they have to pay their rent. But still! Did she ever try to match me up with at least some of my skills? Like for an office job? No! Maybe I could've worked as a cashier taking the money. Maybe as a manager. But managers always end up pitching in if an employee is absent. They would have to flip burgers, mop floors and clean toilets, load stock, and whatever else was needed. Or maybe refer me to a job at the corporate office?

Chapter 3: A Difficult to Understand Spiritual Reading:

Didn't See it Coming

Initially, my winter solstice reading for 2018 was confusing to me.

Metu Neter cards: Het Heru tem maat/ Maat tem maat

I Ching: Hexagram 30

Sacred Path card: 10 West Shield Intersection/Goals

Sacred Contract Archetype: The Addict

Why did it change from an open Het Heru tu maat at the summer solstice to a closed Het Heru tem maat? I thought in terms of spending. I had no other income except the school loan stipend. Yet I spent and lived as if I still have extra money. It may be Maat tem because more people are asking me for my money and my time. I give and then worry that I gave too much. Some people don't or won't do for themselves.

I was exhausted after eight years of grueling graduate school life. So for the beginning of 2019, I needed to take time to rest and to get clarity. I do have more than others in terms of "money" because I save, and my only expensive addiction is buying ebooks. Everyone has an addiction, which is defined

as anything you keep doing despite the negative consequences, you have wanted to change but has been difficult to change, although you have tried.
I also share of my time, clarity and intellect. So how do I know when to share and will not to share? I witnessed people who are used to demanding that other people do almost everything for them. Refusing to follow guidance given to them repeatedly over and over again. Want other people to do the hard work and sacrifices. Stuck in likes and dislikes from childhood.

On the contrary, I have constantly sacrificed my likes and dislikes in order to achieve, which was mostly driven by my desire to heal emotionally and spiritually. Ambition got me a higher education, and previously good paying jobs. But judged by other's standards, I lack material wealth. Yet heaven blesses me with a flow of abundance. What I need just comes, including in the form of money.

But then I started feeling lazy. I didn't feel like pushing myself to do anything. I was recovering from a year of fear, that shook and undermined my confidence in all areas of my life because I'd been rejected again and again for internship clinical training sites. Exhausted. Het Heru can be lazy and extravagant. Yet the Sacred Path card: 10 West Shield Intersection/Goals was advising me that I needed to retreat, rest, have time alone to care for my own health and spirituality. This is the opposite of my usual workaholism. Recent astrological interpretations from the Mercury retrograde, full moons and eclipses explained that everyone was tired, exhausted from the struggles of the hard life lessons of 2018. Most people were begging to rest. There was hope that the new year would bring in lighter loads and freedom. The main lesson of 2018 was to learn who we each really are, our authentic self, and awareness of our true heart's desire.

The winter solstice reading of 2018 challenge of Het Herut tem maat/ Maat tem maat was reminding me not to get depressed and discouraged with the many delays in getting a clinical psychology internship. I finally received approval from my chairperson in August for my clinical research project (CRP) that is similar to a written dissertation. Great, however, the bindery relocated without telling me until two months later, and then announced it would require more time for them to get the printing machines set up and to print my CRP.

On the evening of March 1, 2019, I heard a knock and thud against my apartment front door. Outside was a large box. Inside the box were three beautiful hardcover copies of my CRP! Early as possible Monday morning, excitedly cherishing my success, I rushed a copy to the Dean and assistant dean of the clinical psychology program, for the last signatures of approval. They gave me lots of congratulations for finally obtaining an internship and finishing my CRP.

I took the other copy to the librarian, so she could put it on the back room shelves filled with the other CRP's from many previous years. She mumbled something about, "I don't know what will happen to the students' CRP's if there's no physical campus or program anymore."

And she didn't know what happened to the email for my digital copy of my CRP to be taken to the registrar for final sign off on my transcripts. I sent her the email again, and then rush down to the register's office.

Four days afterwards, on March 7, 2019, my cell phone email chimed with an email from my academic advisor. This was a surprise because he's usually slow to respond to my emails. I had invited him to my presentation at the upcoming ABPSI convention. He wrote that he wasn't going there this year. But then he also wrote: "Not sure if you are in the loop with what was announced today regarding the school, and Friday being the last day of operation. If you have not, please make sure you get copies of all your records. The National Register is offering the opportunity to bank, meaning to store your credentials and items for free. This will allow you to keep a record for the future."

I reread my academic advisor's email. I wondered if I understood it correctly. That the next day would be the last day of Argosy university? All across the United States, Argosy university campuses abruptly closed due to bankruptcy.

I was lucky that I read his email while I was waiting for my psychotherapist that morning, so I could cope with what that could possibly mean. Afterwards, I went up to campus. Everyone was supportive in spite of being in shock and the surreal feeling of the situation.

On Friday, reality set in as I saw empty library bookshelves and empty shelves in the teachers' offices. Boxes, books, litter in the library and the hallways. There were less people on campus than yesterday. Some students I hadn't seen in years. I wandered the halls, frustrated. I ate lunch with two of them. We shared information and strategies on what to do next.

The next day I cried and sobbed as reality began to personally sink in. I went on and went to the Association of Black Psychologists Chicago Chapter meeting, where they had written "ARGOSY STUDENTS" on the agenda. I'm glad I went because otherwise I would have stayed home isolating myself against being around people who would have asked me how I was doing. ABPSI sent emails inviting Argosy students to come in, and they had Argosy University alumni there for support and to validate our experiences at the university. Someone also thought to grab as many bound copies of CRP's by people she knew as possible. I did not think about grabbing mine while I was on campus although I took a few library books I was interested in. The meeting also had lively discussions of relevant current topics that lightened my mood.

Maat is also optimism and faith. How do I manage to have faith and optimism with so many disappointments and delays?

Het Heru did show up in surprising ways. First with creativity, as I started knitting shoes again. One order was for a red and blue pair with only instructions size 8 narrow, high top style, with no preference for either red or blue. So it was left up to me how to pattern the red and blue yarn. I also excitedly began designing and sewing my clothes again, which I hadn't done in 30 years. It was enjoyable with true pleasure and excitement. Somewhat bordering on addiction. Sewing is mostly what I thought about. I would even forget to eat and frequently stayed up late. Here again with Het

Heru, I didn't know if I was spending too much money on fabric and sewing supplies.

I hoped it was okay. Years in graduate school was mostly T-shirts and jeans, without much attention to fashion or appearance. So now I get to dress up.

But sewing at times was also frustrating. I'd forgotten how to sew after all these years. I put my pants together completely wrong. I had to take it all apart and do it the right way. My confidence was shaken, and I began to doubt my abilities in other areas of my life. I finally got brave enough to make a list of what I still wanted to achieve, what were my dreams and goals. With Het Heru energy, her imaginings can become real, and actually manifest in everyday life.

Both positive and negative imaginings will manifest. Angel numbers also reminded me to stay positive and to write my goals. This encouragement gave me such a welcome change from my previous apathy and fear of the future.

Surely as I Ching Hexagram 30, line 3 predicted something good is coming to an end to be replaced by something better. With small miracles along the way and synchronicities, I did somehow believe much better is happening and is in the making. I was distressed the prior two years, because I hadn't matched for an internship. In a few months, I began an internship with all I wanted for clinical training: health psychology, integrative spirituality, and working with children. Who would've known?

Chapter 4: Oshun's Blessings

After I paid $50 for a spiritual reading from a Cuban condomble priestess to tell me, "You already know what I know, so I can't tell you what to do," I wondered what I did know that she and a prior Ifa priest said I knew. Well that was almost 25 years ago and I'm beginning to understand what it is that I may know that they know. This is only because I have begun to listen more, pay attention to the subtle messages that we all get and to follow that guidance. In addition, like a babalou is trained in using the Ifa for 20 years before being considered a babalou, I have been using the I Ching and Metu Neter for 20 years but without a teacher. Experience taught me as I've simply been shown how the readings manifest and describe situations accurately. Note that 50, 25, and 20 are all multiples of five — Osun's number.

Many synchronistic spiritual connections to people and events occur at the Association of Black Psychologists conferences. Perhaps because there are so many high energy powerful spiritual people there. Let me explain:

I'm reminded of a past ABPsi convention, where I was looking for the location of the silent art auction. On the way when I turned into the vendor area, I was surprised to find behind me a table full of tall beautiful African dolls, each unique. The man selling them said, "A woman in Senegal makes them. Earlier a woman saw the dolls, picked up one of the dolls and yelled and cried out. As I observed her, I told her, "Nothing like this has happened before. Later I gave her the doll free of charge."

Hearing him tell me this, I was curious. I said, "I want a doll but not for free." Aware of him observing me, cautiously I went to select a doll. At first, I saw a light peach colored eyelet lace dress on a smaller doll. But her face was not that attractive to me. As I looked up and was about to move on past her to the other dolls on the table, there was another doll that seemed to be looking at me. I couldn't see her dress, only her head. I went over and picked her up. My right index finger traced along each side of the braids with cowrie shells that outlined her face. Then immediately down her back to her ample buttocks. Then up over her shoulder lightly tracing her smaller breasts. Tears came to my eyes in the process. My femininity! Osun is giving me back my sexuality and womanhood! I grabbed her up, holding her close to me.

"This is another one." He told another man as he nodded towards me. He went away for a little while and returned with a small credit card machine and asked slowly, pausing in between each word, "What numbers do you want me to put in here?"

I said, "Five zero. $50 for Osun. Can I have her for $50?"

Silently I thought, if I had $500, I would give it to him. I've seen similar size dolls that didn't have as much detail, costing $300. The price on the tag was $70.

He held his head down as he slowly punched in the numbers.

The other man who was short and round said, "The other woman who chose the doll is a priest. You're a priest too. I knew it the first day when I saw you and saw the circle of braids on the top of your head. Are you a priest?

I said, "Yes, somewhat. Perhaps a closet priest."

He nodded and said, "You could be trained in Africa."

I asked him, "Are you a priest? Do you do Ifa readings?"

He said gruffly, "Yes I'm a priest. I'm a well-known priest."

I ducked a little, mostly from him feeling insulted, but I wasn't ashamed to have not heard of him. And even if I did, I've not been impressed by people's titles. There were many famous people at the conference and I really didn't know what I was supposed to do with them. Do I curtsy and bow as I did in Zimbabwe? Or do I prostrate myself prone on the floor?

He said, " I don't usually do readings, but I will make an exception for you. If you come back at 10 AM tomorrow I will do it for you. What did the doctors tell you was wrong with you? Why are you in a wheelchair?"

I said, "The doctor said it was multiple sclerosis at first but the next month after looking at my MRIs changed it to spinocerebellar degeneration."

He said, "I can consult with other doctors and priests in Africa."

I said, "How much does a reading cost?" I still had my Visa card in my hand. I hoped it wasn't a lot.

He said, "I would have to do a reading to see how much to charge. Wait here."

He came back, stood by the side of a table and threw several coins on the carpeted floor. I saw nichols, dimes, and pennies. The other man reached down and retrieved a stray coin and told him, "Here's another coin."

It was a dime. The priest added it to the other coins and threw them again.

He picked up the coins and turned to me saying, "You have to be honest with me. You have to tell me the truth. Tomorrow you have to tell me the truth."

I said, "I'm usually honest. This year, Ochosi has been working with me, making me aware of when I haven't been honest and of my own unconscious injustices towards other people."

He said, "I know."

Later the other man said, "Tomorrow you have to be honest, tell him the truth, tell him everything. Remember God will be speaking through him. Listen to what he says. It is not the man, as you know him, speaking. It is God speaking through him."

The next day, I waited and waited for the priest starting at 10 AM. I missed some of the conference sessions because of it. I asked the other man if he had seen him. He told me to just go and he will find me when he comes. I checked back later in the afternoon. The priest came and said, "The young woman never came and brought me the cowrie shells for me to do the Ifa reading."

He talked on and on about her. But I doubt that he intended to do the Ifa reading for me after the coins he threw on the floor yesterday told him the truth. He was probably the one who wasn't being honest. When he threw the coins on the carpeted floor of the hotel, he immediately understood its meaning and without an explanation walked away. I went home and did my own I Ching reading. No, to allowing him to help. The main point here is respect for the divine guidance is above our own personal opinions. Osun was initially the only Orisha shown the secret of how to throw the Ifa cowrie shells to divine the future.

I brought the doll home and placed her on the nightstand by my bed. When my Nigerian personal assistant saw her, she put her hand on her chest and wide eyed briefly stepped backwards. "Nana Yeye Osha! Nana Yeye Osha!" she said.

"What's wrong? What's a Nana Yeye Osha?"

"That doll looks just like the wise women who you see in the streets that people give money to. You see what she has in her hand?" She pointed to the large woven straw spiral disc in the doll's right hand. "That's how you know."

"Oh! That's how come the priest told me the doll was special and that I was a priestess too."

Chapter 5: Sekert (Oya's) Influences on My Destiny

Het Heru's personality traits are the opposite of Sekert's traits. I was born on a Saturday. Sekert is also Saturn energy expressed as introverted, a loner, serious, celibate, enjoys solitude, being organized and on time, saves money and can be miserly, with austere or minimal furnishing and clothes, often serious and practical.

Het Heru is outgoing, friendly, social, freely sexual, having to be around people, partying, spending money on beautiful clothing, makeup, hair, home, car and fun. This has made striving to be more like Het Heru challenging.

The day on which you were born describes more of your personality than your astrological sun sign. It is how people actually see you and how you operate in the world. You can go on the internet to find what day of the week you were born on. Simply type in your full birthdate then "day of the week."

Summer Solstice 2021 reading:

Metu Neter cards: Sekert tem tchaas/ Uatchet tu tchaas. I Ching Hexagram 11 Peace and Harmony (lines 3, 4, and 5) into Hexagram 58. Sacred Path card: 13 Coral Nurturing.

Sekert tem tchaas reminds me of my attempts of trying to adjust to being an elder. Sekert is the elder, the old crone. During the months between June and December 2021, I was too busy, too Sekert hyperfocused on whatever task I was doing. Rushing to make little Black dolls and other miniature houses, churches, furniture and scenes in preparation for the Association of Black Psychologists' psychoeducation program, "Family Friendly Suicide Prevention" the first week in December.

The Sekert personality is able to sit still for long hours, patiently concentrating on detailed tasks, sacrificing other needs to meet deadlines of a long-term goal. Tasks that would be too tedious, boring and tiring for most people. One day, I did ask myself, why was I pushing myself through this? It was actually starting to get boring, monotonous and sometimes felt too difficult to problem-solve how to sew tiny doll clothes or insert tiny parts of prefabricated miniature houses when my old hands have a slight tremor and I can barely see closeup items. Hasn't what I've done already enough? Do I have to be such a perfectionist? The next day, my enthusiasm returned as I recommitted myself to finishing. Woke up with ideas on how to repair mistakes or easier ways to do projects. Friends and family also cheered me on by telling what I was making was amazing. One of my sisters told me the dolls have healing energy.

The older we get, hopefully with experience, we have learned that there are often solutions to problems, instead of giving up when make a mistake or are in a crisis. Mistakes or crises often are not as huge or hopeless as our minds think. Just a tiny change can make a great improvement.

Loneliness is a pervasive disease spread globally as a by-product of capitalism and "success." In the United States, the public schools, religions and families often don't teach relationship skills. We need neighborhoods that care about and support everyone, with adults to role-model healthy relationships, problem solving, and show respect for elders and their wisdom. It is a great loss to society when we don't honor our elders and learn from and apply their wisdom.

Uatchet along with Sekert is our unseen Ancestors helping us. Over those past few months, I had more insights, integration of memories, synchronicities, serendipities, and remembered more deep nighttime dreams. This also reflects Sekert and our Ancestors' ability to manifest our daytime dreams, goals, desires and needs.

Sekert is also our destiny and tries to bring us back around to getting back on track. Lately, I noticed I started saying in conversations with others that I was checking items off of my "bucket list." Usually I don't like that term because I'm not that old or ill, but the COVID pandemic reminds me daily that I could be gone any day, and same with people and organizations I know. It is not promised that any of us will wake up tomorrow. Sekert is our awareness and preparation for death and rebirth throughout our lives. Each life transition, even a positive change such as graduation, wedding, pregnancy, births, job promotion, moving to a new neighborhood or city means a small death of leaving behind the old to embrace a desired new adventure. We struggle initially with new situations and are tempted to leave. Sometimes we do leave. Yet, reminiscing doesn't bring us back to how we used to be before a major change. COVID pandemic forced a lot of changes within us, and the environmental around us.

Is it possible that our bucket list begins in childhood? When I was a teenager, I was making several different kinds of dolls. I cut and wrapped copper wire with old cotton brown stockings to make doll bodies. Designed the custom-made dolls for relatives based on their interests. For example, I made a bendable beautifully costumed skater and a ballerina. Made a poster size flute player with brightly colored felt on a burlap background. Later I sewed assorted shades of tans and brown dolls made with Raggedy Ann and Andy sewing patterns. I was spurred on by the fact that multicultural brown skin dolls were rare when I was a child.

I have also wanted to illustrate children's books ever since I was a little bitty girl. At age fourteen, I entered a popular drawing contest in magazines, and won ten dollars. My foster parents bought me a Jon Nagy drawing kit.

Hours and hours I spent teaching myself how to draw faces. I would fill up a whole sheet of paper with just eyes, another with noses, and one with all mouths.

As an adult, I came to Chicago to the School of the Art Institute intending to learn book illustration and computer animation for non-violent video games. Most of my elective classes were figure drawing. Unfortunately, admission to computer classes were based on seniority, so the classes were always filled by the time my turn came to register for classes. Just before I dropped out of art school a senior student advised me to just buy the computer software and teach myself, because that's what he had to do anyway. Computer software cost in the upper hundreds and thousands of dollars at that time. So as much as I tried over the years that didn't happen. I bought some cheap basic computer software but didn't have the time to use it.

Now with new technology, videos and animation is available to the general public, it is cheaper, quicker and easier than 20 years ago, when artists had to use hundreds of hand drawn storyboards to make a movie. You can make a GIF of yourself with just one click. However, life has its detours so fifty years later, life brought me back around to making bendable dolls, and requests for children's books and videos about our ancestors' unseen role in our lives. Sekert influenced by Saturn is slow, real slow, with careers that take off running much later in life. But how slow is slow!

Turning Points

You may remember that with my very first Native American card reading with the Medicine Woman Cards, in 1994, I was advised to made a list of what major events happened every seventh year of my life up to the age of thirty-five years. I went off to college and to Zimbabwe soon afterwards, then returned to the United States to become homeless. Thereafter I was surviving crises, or making life changes that seemed to come faster, and faster than seven years, as I focused on healing. I forgot about turning points, until 2022 while writing this book. To my amazement, looking back I see that major decisions and changes in my life did indeed mostly occur every seventh year:

42 years old: Lived in Zimbabwe

43 years old: Homeless

45 years old: First wheelchair

49 years old: Briefly stayed in an assisted living facility until I got my own apartment

52 years old: Began graduate school master's program

54 years old: Began graduate school doctoral program

64 years old: COVID pandemic. Graduated from doctoral program.

Chapter 6: Healing the Past

Full healing requires attention to all areas of our lives, **physically** (healthy food, sleep, exercise, safe homes and neighborhoods) **emotionally** (all feelings are acknowledged. Be valued and accepted by others in relationships and the community) **mentally** (be able to think clearly, using your skills and talents) and **spiritually** (having faith, a reason for living, peace, harmony and morality).

But how far back in the past do we have to go to heal? Do we ever really die? What if we lived other lifetimes in other cultures, with different genders and skin complexions? Can it really be healed?

A friend introduced me to the Past Life Cards. I decided to buy my own deck, and use the cards to get guidance on what would help me heal my Muslim childhood trauma issues, that I was working through with a Muslim therapist.

Past: **Egypt**. The past life that triggered the situation inquiring about.

May have had a significant past life in Egypt. When a stubborn negative pattern refuses to heal, its roots may be from from a past lifetime. May have an interest in Egyptian culture, spirituality, astronomy, astrology. Or could have feelings of avoiding traveling to the area because of unconscious memories past life traumas from there.

Current: **Trust and Faith.** What you need to know, and to work on right now.

Being able to have faith and trust in the universe, people, and yourself affects your peace and joy in life. May have experienced betrayal in a past life and therefore have difficult trusting other people. The other two cards also influence how much faith you have.

Future: **Communal Living**. What your immediate future could be like if follow the guidance.

Probably lived in a convent, monastery or tribe where your basic needs were provided. Everyone contributed collectively to the community. In your current life you are bothered by an individualistic monetary system and living alone. Have to find a balance between individual and group needs and reach out for help.

My Immediate Impressions and Reflections

First, the photos on the cards are so meaningfully related to my known past history, and current life situation. The Egypt card has a photo of the pyramids. The upside-down middle card has a photo of a statue of an angel. And the last card has a photo of the Anasazi Native American stone dwellings built into the side of a mountain. In my present lifetime my outer appearance is an African American with Native American heritage. A Native American medicine man told me to check out my African culture because it is similar to the Native American culture. I was led to a group of women who practiced traditional African culture, however soon afterwards, I became a member of the Ausar Auset Society Church that is based on Ancient Kamitic now called Egypt's spiritual beliefs. Yet, I never had an interest in visiting Egypt or the pyramids as many African Americans have excitedly done or wish to do. Nor has reading scholarly books on Kamitic history interested me. I did gain passion for studying astrology, but only as it helps us understand ourselves. Not interested in interpreting the stars nor predicting the future. I'm content with letting someone else calculate and read astrology charts.

I lost my trust and faith during this current lifetime's childhood and into young adulthood as my cruel fathers and second husband used religion to abuse us. They had been converted to Islam. Abuse happens in all major religions because people are people, but also conquerors used religions to try to destroy advanced civilized cultures. Indigenous spiritual practices were forbidden, hidden, corrupted, and fragmented into multiple unrecognizable pieces. Angels were once indigenous deities, therefore it makes sense that the middle past life card Trust and Faith is upside down. And central to both African and Native American cultures is communal living. Previously, I had past life memories of being a male chief of a tribe and watching my people leave while I stayed to do what I could to carry on the traditions. Yes, at my core is a deep, deep longing for communal living. I resent that the Romans and later Arab Muslims invaded Egypt and Northern Africa, and that American society forced us to live separately and be competitive, instead of with cooperation and trusting each other. Not even sure if we know how by now.

Chapter 7: The Beautiful Ninety-Nine Names of Allah: Wazifa Card Set

And at last, but not least, making peace with my Muslim upbringing, by finding the beauty in Islam, in the meaning of the ninety-nine attributes of Allah. As a child, I remember seeing a list of the ninety-nine Names of Allah in the back of English translations of the Quran. It took me a while to find it in recent publications, in fact I didn't find a list until the end of the final draft of this book. This was worth the wait, as I found it, and more while reading the book, <u>Physicians of the Heart: A Sufi View of the Ninety-Names of Allah</u>, it immediately brought tears of joy to my eyes. The authors sum up and describe very well our deep internal longing that is usually difficult to put into words. Especially difficult for those who have had near death or other spiritual experiences to describe, and more so for other people who haven't, but struggle with emotional pain and addictions. The deep, deep longing for connection to the universe and each individual's unique purpose in life. The book, <u>Physicians of the Heart</u> has the best explanation I've seen.

The authors wrote from a different Islamic perspective than I've known. Not religious, instead a gentle psychological, mystical, spiritual perspective. All these years, I didn't know that the Quran was actually mostly sounds of words of power similar to mantras, and the Hadiths had stories of the Prophet Muhammad's mystical experiences. I had given up on ever understanding the Quran even in English. Perhaps earlier even if I was told this, I probably would not have understood until after I had my near death experience in 1982. The authors of, <u>Physicians of the Heart</u>, help us all to see and feel that Allah is the essence of pure Love and much more, within and around us. Not a huge man sitting in the sky full of wrath for our sins.

Initially, my goal for studying the list of ninety-nine Names of Allah was to show how Arabic names were perhaps based on multiple "deities," similar to ancient African stories of the different attributes of one God. Further, I wondered if other people also noticed how their birth name's meaning affects their own destiny as their life unfolds. Learning more and more about the meaning of my own name helped me to understand myself better. To my delight, in the book, Physicians of the Heart, I found where my name Haneefa came from. It is based on the Arabic word haneefah referring back to Abraham tradition of believing in the ability to obtain the inner state of unified consciousness of oneness. During my near death experience, I experienced the oneness with total love, peace, acceptance and understanding. When I returned to my body in earthly life, I longed to feel that incredible love and peace again.

The book, <u>Physicians of the Heart</u>, is so named because Sufi healers use the special encoded sounds of the Arabic words of the ninety-nine Names of Allah to heal mental and physical ailments. Most mental disorders are actually spiritual dis-eases of not being connected to the universe and community as one. Each of the Names of Allah invoke and awakens a specific energy the patient needs, for example Ar-Rahman unconditional love and connection, or Al-Jabbar for inner power and strength.

I believe and know the healing potential of sounds of power because I've experienced this myself. For nine years after my near death experience, I prayed pleading for understanding and for what to do with my new way of thinking, seeing, and relating to the world. My prayers didn't begin to be answered until I came to Ausar Auset Society Church where they introduced me to how to have an inner sense of peace through meditation, mantras, rituals, yoga, and better mental and physical health with homeopathy, Ayurvedic and Chinese medicine. These practices helped me integrate and start to make sense of my spiritual and psychic experiences.

An Ausar Auset Society Church priest gave me another name, the Khamitic name AkhiaNeter-t that means, "God is my joy," based on my Metu Neter card Het Heru destiny reading. West Africans and other Africans have a tradition of having naming ceremonies a week after an infant's birth where insight into the baby's destiny is obtained during a ritual, then announced to the gathered community. This is the true meaning of "it takes a village to raise a child." The community learns the child's potential strengths as well as weaknesses to be able to guide the child throughout life. From birth each person is taught to be responsible for their personal growth as well as the whole community's ongoing growth. This is also a Native American tradition, and we acquire more names throughout life as others observe and appreciate our individual talents. When you hear other people say your name, they are invoking energies to assist you. Hopefully, your parents chose names that have meaning.

The ecstasy of connecting to Allah or Oneness is similar to having the overwhelming love, peace and acceptance of a near death experience. Some dreams also give another glimpse of the afterlife or between lives and different dimensions.

I had another natural ecstasy experience in my earthly life when I performed a Het Heru ritual in 1995. On a Friday, dressed in a blessed tie-dyed green and yellow dress, I went down to a river in a small rural town. It was a partly sunny and warm summer day. Singing the Het Heru mantra I offered Het Heru five nectarines, because I couldn't find peaches. I put the nectarines in the water one by one. As I deep breathed and looked at the water, I imagined myself in the river flowing gently over, under, even squeezing around large boulders in the rough waters. To my surprise, I was filled with contagious joy and peace for weeks afterwards.

Similar aftereffects happened when I went another time to a large city river. I again imagined myself flowing with the water. The difference was I didn't have the peaches to offer and it was a cloudy, dreary day and my depressed mood matched the dark weather. Yet, afterwards I still experienced inner joy. These rituals were done alone. Could you imagine the power of a group ritual for Het Heru and other deities' energies?

CHAPTER 7: THE BEAUTIFUL NINETY-NINE NAMES...

<u>Physicians of the Heart</u> explains how invoking any of the specific ninety-nine Names of Allah restores hope and endless possibilities of being able to transcend beyond our present way of how we think about ourselves. Similar to Yoruba Ifa deity characteristics, the authors acknowledge and include the dualities of the natural opposites of virtues. Helping us go beyond the woundedness of shame, worthlessness, and loneliness. Seeking a better life and relief from suffering, we are shown the possibilities of changing and growing spiritually. With the healing practice of invoking of specific names of attributes of Allah it is possible to change our thoughts, moods and behavior. Therefore taking responsibility for our actions to improve the world.

Several of the healing attributes would be useful, making it difficult to choose just one of the ninety-nine Names of Allah. Gratefully, the authors of <u>Physicians of the Heart</u> designed the <u>Wazifa Card Set</u>, so we can pick a card from the deck, and gain understanding. Then go to their website for the correct pronunciation for chanting.

Ninety Nine Names of Allah

The following is a list of the ninety-nine Names of Allah in the order the authors of <u>Physicians of the Heart</u> has them in chapter 5, and also on the Wazifa cards with brief descriptions. For the initial purpose of getting to know more about how one's destiny may be related to one's given name, I've summarized the descriptions into a few words.

But please read the book, <u>Physicians of the Heart</u> for much richer, deeper meanings and healing of which is the original intent of the book.

1). **Rahman**: Unconditional pure Love. 2). **Rahim**: Loving Mercy. 3). **Malik**: Embraced, held, loved. 4). **Quddus**: Purifying, letting go. 5). **Salam**: Peaceful. 6). **Mu'min**: True Faith. 7. **Muhaimin**: Protection from corruption. 8). **Aziz**: Self-worth. 9). **Jabbar**: Power and strength to heal. 10). **Mutakabbir**: Transcendence, growth. 11). **Khaliq**: Creativity, imagining possibilities. 12). **Bari:** Individuation as strive for freedom from faults. 13). **Musawwir**: Towards manifestation. 14). **Ghaffar**: Need for forgiveness. 15). **Qahhar**: Longing for Allah. 16). **Wahhab**: Continued blessings and abundance. 17). **Razzaq**: Gives gifts. 18). **Fattah**: Opening of the heart. 19). **Alim**: Knowing. 20). **Qabid**: Contraction. 21). **Basit**: Expansion. 22). **Khafid**: Slows down. 23). **Rafi**: Raises up. 24). **Mu'izz**: Self-esteem. 25). **Mudhill**: Humility. 26). **Sami**: Listening, hearing. 27). **Basir**: Seeing. 28). **Hakam**: True Wisdom. 29). **'Adl**: Balance and harmony. 30). **Latif**: Deep love and kindness. 31). **Khabir**: Inner knowledge and insight. 32). **Halim**: Tender, nurturing love. 33). **Azim**: Divine presence.

34). **Ghafur**: Total forgiveness as core wound hurt is healed. 35). **Shakur**: Thankfulness. 36). **'Alyy**: Transcendence. 37). **Kabir**: Infinite. 38). **Hafiz**: Protection from fear and despair. 39). **Muqit**: Provider of sustenance. 40). **Hasib**: Accountable and responsible. 41). **Jalil**: Divine power and strength. 42). **Karim**: Generosity. 43). **Raqib**: Devoted loving, deep concentration. 44). **Mujib**: Ask and listen for Allah's answer. 45). **Wasi**: Infinite omnipresence of Allah. 46). **Hakim**: Healing wisdom. 47). **Wadud**: Learning how to love. 48). **Majid**: Unexpected, amazing gifts of abundance. 49). **Ba'ith**: Spiritual awakening. 50). **Shahid**: Witnessing all dimensions. 51). **Haqq**: To be. 52). **Wakil**: Complete trust in Allah. 53). **Qawiyy**: Letting go of the need to always be in control because of fear. 54). **Matin**: Strength of perseverance and integrity. 55). **Waliyy**: Ability to receive unconditional love and to unify. 56). **Hamid**: Gratitude to Allah. 57). **Muhsi**: Knowledge that everything is important. 58). **Mubdi**: To initiate, to begin. **Mu'id:** Returning to the source. 60). **Muhyi**: Giver of life and vitality. 61) **Mumit**: Giver of death. Meaning transformation from the small deaths of one's ego self. 62) **Hayy**: everlasting energy for living. 63) **Qayyum**: continues to exist, to stand. 64). **Wajid**: Manifesting inner ecstasy. 65). **Wahid**: Infinite Oneness. 66). **Ahad**: Unique.

67). **Samad**: Continuous. 68). **Qadir**: Meaning, purpose, potential. 69). **Muqtadir**: Staying on your destiny life path. 70). **Muqaddim**: Patience. All happens at the right time. 71). **Mu'akhkhir**: Completing goals, finishing what you start. 72). **Awwal**: Pure potential. 73). **Akhir**: Already there. 74). **Zahir**: Fully present, fully visible. 75). **Batin**: Unseen calmness, the stillness of existence. 76). **Wali:** Safe and protected in relationships. 77). **Muta'ali**: Pure transcendence progress. 78). **Barr**: Realize that you are perfect, complete and truly loved. 79). **Tawwab**: forgiveness, compassion, including self. 80). **Muntaqim**: balanced reciprocity for deeds, no revenge. 81). **'Afuw**: Complete total forgiveness. 82). **Ra'uf**: Deep, inner, gentle love. 83). **Malikul-Mulk**: Reminded that you are always held in divine love. 85). **Muqsit:** Equal, just appropriations. 86). **Jami:** Integrated connection into whole self. 87). **Ghaniyy**: Fullness with a sense of being and having enough. 88). **Mughni**: Inner contentment, knowing Allah provides. 89). **Mani**: Divine protection, knowing you are safe.

90). **Mu'ti**: balanced receiving and giving. 91). **Darr**: Open your eyes and heart to see your mistakes. 92). **Nafi**: Purification to be able to benefit from the higher good. 93). **Nur**: Light of truth, pure love, wisdom from within. 94). **Hadi**: Awakening to Divine guidance. 95). **Badi**: Remembering to return to your true essence. 96). **Baqi**: Life goes on. 97).**Warith**: Return to oneness. 98). **Rashid**: Using inner intuitive and wise teacher guidance. 99). **Sabur**: Perseverance through to end of spiritual path.

Forgiveness

I decided to pull a Wazifa card. It was card 81 Al-Afuw Total Forgiveness. I was confused what forgiveness has to do with me personally at this time. I asked myself, 'Who do I need to forgive? I haven't felt hurt about what anyone did to me, in a while. There was recent animosity from someone who tended to hold a grudge with everybody. I restrained myself from yelling at her when she yelled at me. Alternatively, I thought of giving her the silent treatment that she sometimes gives to me. Over time, I gained compassion for her and prayed for her healing.

Perhaps, I needed to forgive myself? I did have occasional waves of regrets during the past two months, as I had memories from when I was in my 30s and 40s, I realized that I did the same annoying behavior, that I now have to tolerate from people twenty years younger than I. Like them, I wasn't aware of how my words or actions may have hurt other people and their feelings. Yet, older people patiently put up with my behavior. What could they say or do? They probably did the same to other people, like I did. I found myself saying aloud to the universe, "Wherever you are, this side or that side, I am so sorry. I'm so sorry. I didn't know. Please forgive me."

This was a few weeks later, before I read from the book, <u>Physicians of the Heart</u>'s, Chapter 8: The Family of Divine Forgiveness: A Way to Address Layers of Self-Isolation and

Disconnection. Again, my heart filled with emotion and awe as I read and understood the meaning of each of the four Arabic names for forgiveness: al-Ghaffar, al-Ghafur, at-Tawwab, and al-'Afuw. The authors explain these names in relation to our developmental stages of spiritual growth.

In the beginning stage al-Ghaffar we are not able to consider forgiving because of shock and grief. Replaying the hurt over and over again in our minds. And may make the same mistakes over and over again. However, God's loving grace forgives us again and again.

Next step in the beginning stage is al-Ghafur, when we believe we have committed what we deeply feel is the worst crime or that the worst happened to us by another person, and consequently seems unforgivable. To forgive means to give up the grudge or revenge. Reciting al-Ghaffar and al-Ghafur opens the way to healing the wounds of painful memories and imaginings of revenge or the self-loathing, self-judgement, shame and guilt taking up all of one's thoughts. So that you can give up the grudge or revenge to gain compassion for self and others.

My hardest forgiveness task was to forgive my stepfather and foster father. Especially my foster father because I felt my adolescence and sexuality was stolen from me. They did not allow me to innocently play and explore. For decades, the hurt of feeling that I was way behind my peers in life skills, and would I never catch up, haunted me. As an adult, every time depression, loneliness, flashbacks and painful anxiety surfaced I hurt too much to be able to completely forget and forgive.

My first experience with some success with forgiveness was after I ran away from my second husband. I felt at that time that if he ever came after me, he wasn't going to wake up in the morning. He was the only person I honestly hated. I felt guilty for feeling this way, because I remember my grandmother telling us when I was a little girl, "Do not hate anyone. And God don't make ugly." Me deciding that I may have to kill him, gave me an odd sense of relief. I was already angry at Allah for giving me a second husband worse than my first husband!

After a while though, I did get tired of suffering, thinking of all the horrible cruel things that my second husband did, bringing to the surface constant memories and bodily flashbacks of what my stepfather and foster father previously did to me. I wanted to be able to concentrate and be professionally successful as I was before marrying him. So I decided I would forgive him but mostly for my sake, not his. This was only a few months after the divorce. I was still afraid of him but I wanted me, myself and I, back.

Years later, when a friend told me about the expression, "not letting people live rent free in your head"

I understood immediately because I'd experienced this. After escaping from my second husband, there was no room left in my head to think, plan or create new dreams. I prayed for relief from worrying what he would do next, and from the painful memories of all he had done. My guilt and embarrassment over marrying him so quickly without getting to know him, nor having proper religious counsel, plus being divorced twice made me feel like a failure, and sent me into major depression.

At-Tawwab is a higher stage of forgiveness, when we are able to turn away from focusing on faults of self and others, arguing who's right or wrong, to instead turn towards Allah because Allah is always continuously forgiving you with mercy and blessings. You let go and let God, then you are able to open to joy and ease. This was true for me, although I believed I had turned my back on Allah with anger, I was blessed many times over with whatever I needed. These blessings restored my faith in Allah.

Gradually I came to the understanding on my own, that as I forgave myself, I was able to have compassion for others. Letting go of the grudges I carried for years because somebody said something that I didn't like to me or didn't answer my phone calls. Plenty times I said what I hadn't meant to say or was silent when I should have spoken. One day I observed these mistakes happen frequently when we are tired, then we say and do things that we really don't think or plan to do that hurts other people. We forget, just like children are obstinate, mean, and destructive at nighttime when sleepy, that adults temper tantrums are much worse and have long-term consequences. Like why don't we take ourselves to bed at a reasonable hour?

Perhaps my healing went deeper because my mother in spirit, along with other ancestors and spirit guides took me step-by-step through the stages of grief and forgiveness over the course of several years. They put me in specific situations that I wouldn't have known about or chosen for myself. Allah is truly the best of planners. We do still have free will. Although these were really tough challenging situations that most people would not have entered into, and certainly would not have stayed. I also used the oracle cards and I Ching for guidance in making major decisions, for emotional and spiritual growth that led to perseverance and success. Thanks to the help of psychic mediums at Church of the Spirit for bringing through spirit messages of parents and spouses asking for forgiveness and giving brief advice on doing different now. They also gave encouragement and validated I was on the right path and understanding.

A new psychotherapist also helped me release the last of the effects of past trauma. The details of how this was done is the subject of a forthcoming coming book.

Why I pulled the card, Al-Afuw, makes sense to me now. Al-'Afuw means to completely forgive, to have released and healed the memories of the hurt from one's own heart and mind. A peaceful oneness with all that is. It's been a long journey over my adult lifetime to obtain the freedom of full forgiveness.

Soon after publishing my first book, I felt much lighter as I noticed most of the old feeling memories, thoughts and hurts were gone. Other memoir writers related they experienced similar healing. Forgiveness may be the main theme or message from my books. Hidden from my awareness until nearly finished writing these last chapters.

The authors of the book, <u>Physicians of the Heart</u>'s explanation of these four names for the stages of forgiveness goes much deeper than my simple examples from my younger years. Having to go through a "dark night of the soul" during my middle years on my way to forgiveness, was not easy. Eventually, I surrendered to being able to love and trust the universe to provide, and to heal other people's animosity. In the process, with age I let go of unnecessary fears and worries of what others may think. I still can have momentary traces of a hurt, bruised ego. Most of this forgiveness process I learned on my own. I wish that we had the community support that indigenous cultures and traditional Sufism had for emotional and spiritual growth. And wish I had the book, <u>Physicians of the Heart</u> sooner, because I learn more each time I read or reread it, as it still touches my heart.

CHAPTER 7: THE BEAUTIFUL NINETY-NINE NAMES... 113

Sufism

Intrigued by this different perspective of Allah and the Quran, as pure love and healing sounds, I'd like to learn more about Sufis. Particularly to learn about the "guru" process to help students prepare for and while they're in a natural ecstatic state, but most importantly afterwards, to aid them through the immense changes in consciousness and thinking that results in major life transitions.

Many people think meditation is for staying calm, but when you meditate regularly you see the truth of situations. Regardless of how others are swept up in popular illusions and lies, you can no longer. This causes temporary inner discomfort and confusion along with conflicts in relationships because family, friends, coworkers don't want their bubble burst.

I wanted a personal guru but never had one. There is a saying, "When the student is ready the teacher will appear." So I became my own guru and decided one day I would be a guru for others. Several people asked me to be their spiritual counselor, however they weren't invested in doing their personal development work. They either just want to talk, get advice they mostly didn't follow, or they would ask me to do spiritual readings for yes or no answers. I'd rather help students who are dedicated to improving their own life and others, and who will eventually be able to do their own spiritual work.

A friend from Senegal in 2019, introduced me to some of the cultural aspects of Sufism, when she told me about Sheik Ahmadou Bamba. Later, I learned about women contributions to Islam, honestly astonished because we rarely heard about woman scholars or mystics. <u>Wrapping Authority: Women Islamic Leaders in a Sufi Movement in Dakar, Senegal</u> is about Sufi women's religious participation and spiritual leadership. Senegal is located in West Africa and has a 96% Sufi Muslim population. Another book is, <u>Women of Sufism: A Hidden Treasure: Writings and Stories of Mystics Poets, Scholars and Saints</u>, is about Muslim women's contributions from other countries.

There is much more I want to learn about true Islam and the deeper spiritual meaning of all religions. I'm starting to see what my mother loved so much about Islam. How her introducing me to Islam when I was a child, influenced who I am now in fulfillment of my destiny.

Chapter 8: Facing Death and Loss

Many people are afraid of death in the United States and won't talk about it, although there's been a pandemic for almost three years. The only way I hear people talking about death is when they tell friends and family that if they don't get vaccinated they're going to die. Tired, wary of burying their loved ones, they wonder why it's not in the media that death wasn't from COVID, it was cancer, heart attacks, strokes, murders and suicides.

One aspect of Sekert, that I have been a bit afraid of, started with my aunt when I lived with her, there was a pattern of getting to know people for only a couple of years during which they feel an intense need to talk about their lives, guilts, and regrets to me, and then somehow I'm surprised when they pass away shortly after that. This happened with my foster mother who I had not seen in almost thirty years, we got close although it was just with phone calls, and then she passed away. Same with a couple of neighbors, one that I mentioned in the first book that I wrote, <u>Mother's Love from Beyond</u>, we had great love for each other. To the end, James thought he was going to get better, just have physical therapy and come back home. When he was in intensive care, he cried and said he didn't want to leave me. He died two days later. This made me not want to make any more friends with my neighbors in my apartment building since most of them are older than I am.

Perhaps it is my calling, my life purpose, especially since I had a near death experience to help people during their end of life transitions, and to assist families with grieving. Instead, I've avoided this assignment. During the COVID pandemic, I've had to step up to comfort more and more friends and family members. Most people were dying of other causes such as heart attacks, strokes, and cancer. The media's extreme focus on COVID leaves many people isolated, not knowing what to do, and grieving on their own without a nation wide effort to provide support.

Being born during a Saturn period meant lots of other types of losses throughout my life. Writing my memoirs was emotionally challenging, as I realized the World Issues Program at the School for International Training closed the year after I graduated, the ORAP college closed temporarily, and decades later Argosy University closed just before I was about to graduate. All due to impending global financial crises. It was a shock to see that Lowry Air Force near Denver Colorado where I received technical training was long gone. It's not like I can show future generations these locations and say 'Look, that's where whatever used to be.'

Sekert is also our ability to manifest. Usually we think of manifesting as picturing what we want. But whatever we dwell on, daydream about, even negative thoughts can also come true. Knowing this, helped me understand the next part of my summer solstice 2021 spiritual guidance reading: I Ching Hexagram 11 (lines 3, 4, and 5), into hexagram 58. Sacred Path card: 13 Coral Nurturing.

I Ching hexagram 11 Peace and Harmony means a time of social harmony, peace and sharing of prosperity, knowledge and influences. Fighting ends.

Line 3: Changes in the natural cycles of life are to be expected. Therefore prosperity will decrease with time, some evil and disagreements return but you shouldn't become sad. Maintain inner peace and enjoy what you have.

Line 4: Be neighborly without boasting of what you have.

Line 5: Uniting with others and being on same level keeps the peace.

Hexagram 58 is similar to Het Heru concept of Joy. Joy that comes from within in. Joy is a choice. Reach out for joy. In life there is both good and bad. It is possible to have both good and bad experiences happening at the same time. When I look back on my younger adult years I really did not know what joy or happiness was.

My Het Heru destiny to fulfill is to know joy and experience joy. Although I usually identify my inner feelings as calmness, this past year many people described me as joyful.

How do I maintain joy when the COVID pandemic and the climate change crises gives me, probably most of us, lots to worry about as we read articles, listen to and watch news media, plus our own experiences and observations. I saw a PBS special documentary about Jesus and what life was like during his time, with the old struggle of good versus evil cruelty. To my embarrassed surprise, there was then the new idea of apocalyptic events to come and save us all. I have to admit that the idea of an apocalypse gives me comfort. Such as, in the back of the book, Phoenix Rising, is a list of predictions that were given back in the 1980s by an elder Native American medicine woman. Most of these predictions have come true during the past three decades. Natural disasters, freak accidents due to carelessness, a description of Trump-like leaders, with near misses of Third World War (WWIII) and threats of nuclear exchanges. Also the COVID-19 pandemic is mentioned in the book, <u>Phoenix Rising</u>, including the possibility that there could be a man-made accident from a lab. Could COVID-19 be that? Especially since we keep getting contradictory information from the CDC about COVID-19 and the vaccinations effectiveness. We have all been exposed, double exposed, and overexposed to the "virus." So shouldn't we all have herd immunity naturally by now? The elder medicine woman also predicted that people will refuse to go to work because there are no longer any benefits, not even a living wage. Hence, "the Great Resignation, Lying Flat, and Quiet Quitting." Could the chaos of the Trump administration have been staged on purpose to entertain, distract, shield the public from reacting to how serious our domestic and global economic and food shortage problems are? The consequences of overconsumption, treating the environment and essential human labor as disposable.

Sekert also represents the foundational structure of buildings, projects, organizations and society. If the foundation is not correctly built or maintained it will collapse. We've hurriedly thrown together buildings and programs, that now can't be sustained. Sekert is Time. Time to learn from our mistakes, and start from scratch erecting new sustainable, healthy communities.

Although this feels stressful going through major changes, it is amazing to watch all of these Native American predictions unfold, each event bringing us closer to the end days of true peace, equality, and harmony with the environment. While we may arrive kicking and screaming, I can see this new era happening in my lifetime.

I've made a commitment to reviewing my solstice spiritual readings once a week on Saturdays (Sekert's day). Otherwise, with a busier schedule I have less time to remember and focus on my spiritual goals. What I've needed or desired, including finances simply shows up without me doing rituals or even praying for it. Perhaps these are rewards for living life correctly, with guidance from my solstice readings, intuition, and attempts to live out the principles and personalities of the ancient Khametic Paut Neteru deities, saints, attributes of Allah, and wise descriptions of totem animals' behaviors to the best of my understandings.

The other commitment I made, is developing my mediumship skills. Sekert aids in the connection between the Earth and the unseen heavenly world of the Source of pure love, knowledge, and ancestral spirits who have passed on, and those waiting to be born. Sekert is our ability to communicate with our spirit loved ones, enlightened ancestors (Shepsu) and spirit guides. Psychic mediums and indigenous traditional healers are able to relay these messages.

Chapter 9: A Friend Responds Through a Medium Message

My first book, <u>Mother's Love from Beyond: A Healing Journey of Grief and Loss</u>, tells the story of how I was introduced to the concept of mediumship. After it was published, I received the following message in September 2020, during a private reading on the phone with the medium Cher:

"So do we have a question to start with?"

"We do! There is a friend that I have not seen or heard from in a long time, and she lives in another country. I've wondered how she is. She came to me in a dream the other night."

"Okay, what's her first name?"

"Inviolatta."

"That's pretty. Do you think she's made her transition?"

"I've been thinking not yet, but now that you asked, I'm not sure I get that feeling."

"Okay, because when you said her name, right away a woman's face came in with a big smile. Would it be appropriate that she would wear some sort of headdress? Not a hat but some sort of head dress that would cover her forehead?"

I hesitated before answering. "Does it look similar to a cloth beret?"

"I get more of a wrap around her forehead. Not so much like a French beret but more like if I were to wrap my head in a scarf. I would cover my forehead and then I would wrap the rest of my hair."

"Maybe."

"Because I'm getting this woman coming through with a big smile. A headdress, that's what she's calling it. I'm also seeing hoop earrings on her. I get the feeling that maybe the headdress is more about her returning to nature. Returning to her natural state. I don't know if she would have dressed like this per se, but kind of symbolic of returning to a starting point. Does that make any sense?"

CHAPTER 9: A FRIEND RESPONDS THROUGH A... 133

"Yes"

"Do you remember the woman at church who was a naturopath? She moved back home to Africa. This puts me in mind of your friend. This does very much feel like your friend."

"I'm glad."

"I'm asking her to give me a little bit more to identify her. She's got lots of books around her. And I feel like this person was very curious. She had so many interests. Now she's showing me herbal plants. This is where her interest have taken her. She's working with herbal plants. Does this fit at all?"

"Yes. You can keep going."

"All right, but it's hard if I don't hear from you to know if I'm on track."

"Well, you know me. I am able to put the pieces together."

"Right. I do get her being very, very happy. So when you asked how she was doing, she's coming through very happy. She's showing me bare feet."

"Yes!" I said excited.

"I'm hearing 'bare feet and grounding.' Did she work with you on your feet? I feel like she wants to continue. She's saying she wants to continue. She's sending you energy as if she is actually working on your feet. She comes in and I get her putting her hands on your ankles. So in spirit she's a very powerful healer. This may have been more of an interest on this side. But she's really blossoming on the spirit side. And she's a wonderful healer. She comes in and she has her hands on your ankles. I see your feet. She sending you wonderful wonderful healing energy. So it's not so much about her but what she brings for you at this time.

I'm also getting a lot of music coming in. There's a lot of drums. It's not really a Congo drum. They are using the word tribal drum. And the music is really wonderful. It's very uplifting. So she just comes in with a lot of, the word is native, a lot of native energy for you. And I see that energy traveling and moving up into your shoulders and down your arms to your hands. This is a real transfer of energy from her to you. And I feel like, as we know with your work that — oh that's interesting — lot of your healing energy is with words and thoughts. She centers this energy from the heart chakra into your hands. So I feel like this has to do with your writing now. And I hear the word collaborate. She's going to be someone who will be collaborating with you.

"Oh wow!"

"Very, very powerful what comes through. So I see you writing but then it feels like you get stuck and it could be, I'm not sure how to express this. You're not happy with something that you've written and that's when she comes in. She's showing me she's pulling apart some threads. You know, like how knitters roll their yarn into a ball to keep it from getting tangled up?"

"Yes."

"She is coming to help you detangle your thoughts so that you can express it the exact way that you want it to be.

This is going to be fun! (Laughs). That's what she says, 'This is going to be fun.'

There is a real sense of sisterhood that comes through with her."

"Yes, very much."

"There is a strong sense of sisterhood. I feel like the work you were going to be doing with her, as the vibration expands, it is going to bring to you more sisters. That feels really good. And that happens on both sides. She has a couple of sisters that she works with, and she will bring them through when she needs to. But for you, on this side, that vibration is going to bring in more sisters and that feels really good.

"Yes."

"Do you share your writing while you're creating? Do you talk to people about what you're doing?"

"I have, if I know what you mean. I don't share exactly what I'm writing. But this has been different for me because I usually do things alone. I have told people that I'm writing my book and somewhat about the process. Yes, I have found that discussing it actually helps me get more clarity."

"She's showing me something like a writers' workshop, where people are sitting in a circle. It's another type of collaboration as writers talk about their process. So she brings that in for you. Certainly doing something on Zoom could be easier than meeting in the flesh. Discussing the process feels like the most important. Just being with other people. I think a writer's life can be lonely. Can be very singular. And so she brings in this workshop idea so that you again are in community with other people. There is a wonderful exchange of ideas. Not so much of ideas of what you are writing about, but talking about the craft. That's her word, talking about the craft. And that just feeds you. Finding other people like you, other writers gives you energy for what you want to do."

"Now she's bringing in small oranges. I don't know if these are mandarin oranges but they are that size, maybe a little bit smaller. When you take a bite, it energizes you. So she brings that in for you."

"Okay."

"Are there bright colors in your apartment?"

"Yes."

Good. It is important to have bright, bright colors. I'm getting a beautiful yellow coming in. I'm getting a red with some blue in it so it's not a harsh red, but a kind of softer red. And then an orange color. I don't know if that would be the combination. I'm not sure if it's a painting or a fabric but she's bringing in those colors for you. It feels like, especially with winter coming that you, the word is 'need.' You are going to need to have bright, bright colors around you."

Cher was quiet for a few minutes trying to see what else, then she continued, "I feel like we get stuck. It is winter and I feel like I'm stuck. She really wants you to look at how do you take care of yourself. But I don't know if this stuck is more emotional with your writing or physically stuck with the weather. It seems that with winter coming it's going to be more difficult this year. I want to take a long sigh." (Cher makes a big sigh, deep breath sound, and then laughs).

I too sigh loudly.

"After this summer."

"Right."

"We're going to be stuck some more and it is going to be like yeah. So having some bright colors around you is going to be helpful. And I want to have around you some things that you enjoy looking at. And it feels like you have these items but they may be put away like in a cupboard or something."

Yes."

"Leave a couple of things out that bring you joy when you look at them. She's really working to set you up for wintertime because it feels like it's going to be a long one. Long but productive. So that's something to look forward to. I get your friend leaving now and someone else is coming in."

Reflections on the Medium Message

It wasn't until later in the year that I found an old Facebook messenger message from a mutual classmate reported that Inviolatta had passed away two years prior, because I only occasionally go to my Facebook page and didn't know I had to sign up separately for Facebook messenger. Although I had not received emails or letters from Inviolatta for more than two years, in my mind was the possibility that she was still alive. Power outages were frequent when it rained, so it was not unusual for there to be no phone or internet access. Snail mail took months and wasn't secure. Zimbabwe had economic problems, with civil unrest and hearing reports of people being tortured or killed for any disagreements with Mugabe, would've been dangerous for Inviolatta and I to exchange emails.

Inviolatta previously worked for years as a schoolteacher, then later a school principal. Hence, the psychic medium Cher seeing her with books. Later

Inviolatta changed to doing community work through ORAP that included administrative duties of balancing the books. Then she came to the United States to go to the School for International Training (SIT) to get a bachelor's degree from the World Issues Program. That's where I met Inviolatta.

Inviolatta gave me a going away party and her nephew video taped us dancing. She danced in her bare feet. On the SIT campus in the United States, Inviolatta sometimes wore a braided wig, after she had tried to get a perm that made some of her hair fall out. So the next year, at home in Zimbabwe she had very short natural hair. I've not seen her wear a headdress, nor traditional clothes.

What is amazing about this mediumship reading is the message applies more to winter 2022, than the original predictions for 2020-2021. I reviewed the audio recording of the message as I was writing in this second book about Zimbabwe and now understood why I frequently felt Inviolatta's presence, helping me to remember. With my first book in 2020, my writing flowed, and I finished a major draft in six months. Writing in 2022, about my Zimbabwe experiences I felt stuck, as it was challenging to put into words and also emotionally difficult because I miss everybody there. Zimbabwe is my second home.

The writer's workshop idea? Well, I wanted an African American editor this time, who would understand or at least be willing to learn about African American, Native American and other indigenous cultural beliefs and spirituality. Two Black writers' editorial companies turned me down, one editor saying that she wasn't comfortable with the "occult." Occult? Astrology and divination are the occult? The good thing is one of websites offered a Black writer's group. A commitment is required to attend regularly. There is a small annual fee but for me it was worth it.

The COVID-19 pandemic partial shutdown, mask mandate, and social distancing continued into 2022. I really couldn't complain much about the six months full lockdown in 2020. But it's now two years and counting! Cher knew that I usually get mild depression, mostly less smiles in the wintertime because using a wheelchair limited my independent travel outside when it snowed. Literally stuck in the house.

My new couch in my living room is a burgundy red, with two large off-white pillows with a few thin red and orange stripes. Cher hasn't come to my apartment and I hadn't told her about my furnishings. The cloth slipcover, at that time, was a bright red. Later after this message from Inviolatta, I sewed a yellow cover to replace it with a waterproof fabric I already had, but planned to hide it underneath the bright red cover. The yellow cover still brightens my home year round.

Stored away in boxes in my bedroom are my large watercolor paintings. Frames that size can be expensive. A neighbor offered to hang them for me when I first moved here sixteen years ago. But then I went to graduate school, within ten years tall bookshelves covered my walls instead of pictures. This past summer, a colleague Denise came to deliver a big box with the little dolls and miniatures I made for a play therapy demonstration. She visited a little while. Seeing my large sunflower acrylic paintings propped up on some boxes in a corner in the living room she got excited and inquired if I had more. I pulled out some of my paintings and showed her. Denise loved the bright colors and said, "I have frames at my house and am happy to help you hang your paintings. She also fussed at me. "Our creativity needs to be where we can see it. Even if you tape it up on the wall."

Probably a message through my colleague from Inviolatta then, as I'm now reminded that I painted a picture of one of Inviolatta's favorite flowers and gave it to her while I was in Zimbabwe. In one of my boxes is also a large painting of the Zimbabwe flag and other symbols.

In the backyard of her beautiful ranch style home, Inviolatta had a small garden. However, as far as I know she only grew collard greens, not herbs. If she knew about herbs, she didn't talk about them. Her parents and family lived out on the farm in the rural villages, so it is possible that perhaps by watching her mother and other elders she learned about herbs.

The woman wearing white who knows herbs, may be the traditional healer

Leticia, that I studied with in the city. I wore white when I went to the clinic at her house, in a room filled with shelves of jars of herbs and other medicines. But she too had short natural hair and didn't cover her hair. She showed me how to play special tribal rhythms on her drums. Maybe Leticia passed over into spirit too.

It is possible that the headdress, that Cher saw, was only symbolic to help her identify that my friends were African. And Cher remembering our mutual friend from church the naturopath, helped identify what country in Africa, although Cher did not mention Zimbabwe.

My lower legs hurt with the cold and dampness of winter. The pain seems worse this year, especially from my ankles to my knees, as I've made the commitment to exercise and try walking forward with a normal heel to toe gait. I did pray for relief and to have my dream come true of me being able to go hiking again out in nature. In a recent mediumship practice, someone else saw a woman they identified as my mother, was massaging my feet and legs! My legs do feel better.

I'm grateful to have help and encouragement from spirit writing this book. A different main spirit guide, who is precise with words and grammar is leading. I don't argue I just follow. All I know is, this was not my usual way of writing, but I like this no nonsense style. It's easier.

Chapter 10: Ochosi Revisited

In the process of writing this book I reread, <u>Ochosi: Ifa and the Spirit of the Tracker</u>. I was curious how the Ifa reading that the Candomble priestess Valdeci gave me in 1996, about Ochosi energy ruling my head, has influenced my life.

Ochosi protects the needs of the environment. In Zimbabwe, I witnessed elders' knowledge of elemental spirits in everything including the weather. Climate change is a result of all of us improperly using natural resources. Traditional healers knew how to restore balance in the environment. Their drumming brings rain during drought. Spiritual evolution is defined as being in perfect harmony with nature. Ochosi teaches us that everything in nature has a conscience.

My affinity for Native American culture may also be influenced by Ochosi's connection to Native American spirits and the people who are guardians of the land. Animals, especially birds have been my allies, giving me support, encouragement and lightening my mood. Red-winged blackbirds whom I hadn't seen in a few years now make their presence known again as they sing, then fly in front of me, similarly with bright red cardinals and their families, robins, ravens and hawks.

I really miss being out in nature and want to get serious about cabin retreats or even living again out in the countryside, in spite of having used a wheelchair and the COVID pandemic crisis. It may be possible that I won't need the wheelchair outside. I don't know, I haven't tried walking long distances beyond my apartment, nor up and down stairs or uneven terrain yet.

Ochosi gives us knowledge of the mysteries of plants. On my bedroom wall, I have a picture of George Washington Carver for inspiration. Plants talked to him and he listened. Sometimes before sleep at night, I would ask for a dream showing me what foods or natural herb I needed to heal symptoms I was having. Upon wakening, I would write down or draw a picture of what plant I saw in the the dream, and then go research it. Othertimes, books would open to pages of homeopathic medicines needed for someone else.

I did not know back in 1996, why the Cuban priestess gave me the cleansing herbs specifically customized for me. I simply followed her instructions for how to mix them with water and pour this over my head while standing in the bathtub. Nor what it meant for Ochosi's spiritual herbs to open human access to communication with the spirit realm. Nor did I know about mediumship then. I did learn a little about herbal remedies, gemstones, and baths for physical healing, but not about the cleansing herbal baths for spiritual healing that relieves psychological distress. Homeopathy is the closest I've gotten to using herbs to relieve psychological distress.

Thinking about it now, perhaps referrals to priests for the Ochosi spiritual cleansing herbs could open the way for my clients who do not have the capability to be introspective, to have personal insights relevant to changing their behavior, or to see the larger perspectives of how their consequences also affect others. Not everyone is able to think abstractly and apply what they learn verbally with talk therapy.

In my first book, <u>Mother's Love from Beyond</u>, I mentioned I started in mediumship classes at the Church of the Spirit. However I stopped due to transportation problems, and after seeing curriculums for mediumship classes are mostly about spiritualism history. My African and Native American heritage already believes in spirits of our ancestors, so why have to read so many books to prove that life continues after so called death. It's like having to memorize Columbus and other European explorers' history for discovering countries that existed long before they were born! Plus my head is full from textbooks giving me a trillion words vocabulary and theories from years of graduate school. I want real mediumship practice! For now my spiritual guidance messages are admonishing me to get serious about committing to deeper levels of development for being a Seer and Healer. To learn the herbs as well as put more meditation and dreamtime into my daily life.

Ifa and Ochosi's Role

Ifa is a complex system of divination based on the concept of destiny and good character. You chose your destiny before you were born. Balance between self and the world is the basis for developing good character through spiritual transformation. Using divination helps you to be able to make the correct decisions at the crossroads. Consulting the Ifa oracles or a priest for which path to take and following that guidance will bring blessings from the Orisha because of your ongoing good character. Then obstacles will be removed from your path. These obstacles can be internal fears, doubts, confusion, ignorance, inexperience or the wrong motivation. External obstacles are injustice, oppression, poverty, natural disasters, personal illness, and misfortunes. It is important to know the difference between problems caused by your own internal obstacles such as your own thoughts, actions and behavior instead of only blaming external factors.

Ochosi is one of the Ifa orisha energies that can provide you personal guidance and clarity on how to heal and release fears and limitations that hold you back, as well as bring liberation and protection from societal injustices and laws. Similar to Ogun, he has the power to clear away obstacles that are in the way of your spiritual growth. Ochosi's role is to show us the the shortest path to our spiritual goals. Spirit certainly has presented me with inspiration by frequent, awesome miracles that show me the way and to keep me going forward with the hard life tasks.

Remembering the story the priestess Valdeci told me about how Ochosi was initially the warrior Ogun, who had to adapt his hunting method from using a machete, to using a bow and arrows in the Americans, I was really surprised to find a large bow with arrows at a store in downtown Bulawayo, Zimbabwe. Seeing it as a symbol of both African and Native American cultures, I bought it. The bow seemed delicate. However, when I shipped it to my sister's home, and complained because I wasn't allowed to carry it on the plane, she laughed at me,

"A bow and arrow is a weapon after all!" This was before September 11, 2001, so it never occurred to me that airport security would consider me, or the bow and arrows dangerous.

"It Doesn't Matter Where You are Going. Any Road Will Do." Ifa Proverb.

This proverb reminds me of people I know, who come to me for help because they feel stuck, not able to move forward in their lives. Anxiety and fear of failure keeps them from their goals. American society makes these fears worse by pretending to offer numerous opportunities to choose from, yet fierce competition and discrimination only allows a few to succeed, even if your capabilities are the best of the best. More and more information is piled on for what each individual is expected to know. Weighed down, it is difficult to have confidence in making decisions.

As a healer and counselor, I do a lot of prayers on clients' behalf. I ask for heavenly guidance to show me a different way to help heal them. Honestly, sometimes I get frustrated. It can be difficult for me to understand and have empathy when some clients are the complete opposite from me. No inner faith or optimism to pull them forward on their own during tough situations. Not feeling connected to anyone or a higher power, when they pray they feel nothing happens.

Nonetheless, I've been driven to help them to see their hidden potential and beauty. Most importantly, to show them that they are not helpless and therefore can begin taking responsibility for their participation in their own life. To truly accomplish this, supportive spiritually healthy families, communities, and countries are needed. Indigenous cultures understood that we are not meant to do everything alone. Together we have opportunities to improve our character by observing each and everyone around us, naturally showing us a mirror reflection of opposite qualities that we can develop in ourselves and appreciate everyone for being who they are.

The Ochosi book gives warnings to people who refuse to put serious effort into finding their own personal destiny and improving their character. Some people come to me for help but are very reluctant to following through on recommendations so that they can know what faith, peace, joy, and having a life purpose feels like for themselves. They suffer with depression, focused on not having achieved societal expectations of material and career success. Their time is consumed with cellphones, computer games, and television. Rarely having quiet solitude for creativity, sleep and dreaming to connect to self and the universe. Mostly they are afraid of possible loneliness, intense emotions and memories that need to be felt and acknowledged to be healed. Not knowing that underneath these uncomfortable emotions are peace, joy and connection. In contrast, I probably overdo solitude. It is because of my faith and optimism, even the tiniest amount, that I am able to persevere.

Ochosi helps put you on the shortest route to be in perfect alignment with your destiny. A destiny with lessons you agreed to learn in this lifetime before your birth. Well, to say, Ochosi "helps" is putting it mildly, because you will often find yourself in places and situations you hadn't consciously intended to go. I have mixed feelings and opinions about Ifa being based on the belief that when you are focused on developing a good character then you will receive the blessings of a long life with abundance and wealth — while those who have bad characters will be cursed by illness, poverty and infertility. It begs the question, why do bad things happen to good people?

This Ifa and other similar major religions' beliefs in divine punishments, is probably the feelings most people have when Ochosi's energy removes people, activities, and possessions that are not in line with your spiritual destiny path. However afterwards, Ochosi also gives inspiration, guidance, and opens the way for forging a new path that is much smoother and abundance filled. During the ignorance of my younger years, I had more crises that may not have necessarily been due to me having a bad character back then. Mostly, I just didn't know any better, although I adhered to religious rules. My life got progressively better as I committed to following divine guidance from consulting the oracles, and allowed spiritual transformations to happen to the best of my ability. Then as promised, the magic and blessings of Ochosi continues to awe me with abundance and miracles.

Carryover Soul

When I first read of the concept of a "carryover soul" in the books, <u>Spirit Song</u> and <u>Phoenix Rising</u>, I sobbed aloud. A carryover soul is usually thought of as the reincarnation of a grandparent in a later grandchild. West Africans believe similar. It could also represent some of the memories of ancient past lives that intrude on our present lives. I cried because this explained the loneliness I've felt as if I did not belong anywhere, felt so different than my family or anyone else, especially with my strong interest in indigenous spirituality and healing, love of and connection to nature, and how cramped I feel living in cities.

Lonely too, because those who have Ochosi energy will be sabotaged by those closest to us. Ochosi brings us the truth of who hinders our growth and who supports it. Acknowledging this truth was very painful. Since the Cuban priestess explained to me about Ochosi's task to always keep me on a cleared spiritual path means losing those dear to me, I've had less incidences of being sabotaged by those closest to me. Perhaps it is also because I've lived alone for the past sixteen years. And I'm more aware and observant of people who come into my life who only seem to focus on their own needs. Actions speak louder than words, became my motto. Therefore,

I must first become aware of my own thoughts and behaviors that may be leading the other person on. What are my own motives? Am I over giving? Is it a habit of automatically giving or being sucked in to solving other's problems without realizing it?

I am the one who has to know my own intentions, make my actions match my intentions, and then allow others their natural consequences. I had to learn to stop rescuing people from their own choices and behaviors. Sometimes though, following and submitting to my I Ching guidance, means putting up with individuals that I know does not have my best interest in mind. At least, knowing ahead of time that they may cause me to lose or sacrifice something. Usually it is a minor loss.

Where I probably experienced almost nonstop sabotaging, was trying to get through the clinical psychology doctoral program. I learned the hard way that although I spoke up for other's rights, justice doesn't always bring desired results. Even after I transferred to another university the dean and staff "kept losing my documents." A friend commented near the end, "Maybe all these challenges are telling you that maybe you could be barking up the wrong tree."

No, I knew I was to graduate, so I hung in there anyway because I checked in regularly with the I Ching, and Sacred Path, and Metu Neter cards readings along the way. Ochosi, Ogun, and Sekert energies combined gave me the ability to see and understand the bigger picture of the effects of economic decline, discrimination and racism factors to have the strength and courage to persevere. Of course, I asked the I Ching before I submitted my application to the university. The I Ching message was, that going through the doctoral program would mean by my being able to sacrifice for the benefit of helping others, I would reap rewards. I thought that meant that I would see abundance after I graduated with a huge income but to my surprise, I was given all that I needed materially and spiritually, along with family emotional support throughout the program. And much more after I graduated.

Ochosi is our ability to defend ourselves. I've taken a few self-defense workshops for women, a Tai Chi class and now do Qigong for exercise.
But I've not had martial arts classes. Sometimes I tried to imagine how I would have defended myself while sitting in my wheelchair. Could I use the same tactics and strategies to throw a potential attacker off their feet? Perhaps I haven't thought much about physically having to defend myself, because when I call on Ogun (Heru Khuti) energy to surround me with protection and I'm usually safe in my travels.

We are also warned against having narrow minded expectations of quick solutions for how we want wealth to manifest. Ochosi energy is the wisdom, adaptability, flexibility and problem-solving capabilities for survival. Ability to stay focused on a goal, similar to how a hunter has to sit or stay motionless waiting for the right opportunity and time to advance. Transformation always takes place, one step at a time in slow steady increments that requires patience and persistence. In the United States, where we are used to immediate gratification expecting an instant fix, we may miss the many miracles around us. Spiritual growth requires consistent concentration, determination and patience maintained over several years. However, there are times when Ochosi does bring instant transformation, with instant changes in perception that penetrate to the deeper levels of your awareness and consciousness. Those overnight insights, epiphanies and "Ah hah moments" during the day that suddenly connect your understanding of your past, present and future.

I mentioned earlier in Volume 1, about Heru Khuti's ability to assess what is obsolete and no longer needed, Ochosi also pushes us to evaluate and discard habits and items that are no longer working in our lives. This includes getting rid of clutter.

Chapter 11: Getting Rid of Clutter

After living in this apartment building for almost 17 years, in April 2022 I had an extra push, probably from Ochosi energy, to discard old items that I didn't use. The new building owners informed us that they were going to rehab the whole building. New bathroom and kitchen cabinets, countertops, stove, refrigerator, laminate floors instead of carpets, paint, blinds, toilet, and lighting. This would be done five apartments at a time starting with the 11th floor.

They would put us up in a nearby hotel for a week, in my case two weeks because I live in an ADA accessible apartment, and give us a gift card of $180 for meals each week. The hotel would provide the usual continental breakfast, but because of the pandemic their restaurant was closed so we would have to order in, or go out to nearby restaurants. Using Door Dash would use up my money in a few days. The ADA accessible apartments were to be done last, in April, which I was grateful for because my wheelchair wouldn't go through the snow. With the continental breakfast being full waffles, toast, cereal, and mostly fast food joints in the college campus area, I had to go hunting for healthy gluten-free, and vegetarian food.

Friends asked me if I was excited about the move. I had mixed feelings because of course, who wouldn't want a clean new apartment? The catch was although the owners originally told us that movers would come and pack us up, they later told us that the movers would only come on our move out day. They supplied the cardboard boxes, tape, bubble wrap, and packing paper. This is a low-income senior building with a few middle-age people with disabilities, how were we to pack ourselves? Our newest manager, after a secession of managers, informed us at a meeting that we would get fined if our apartments weren't left clean on moving day! She told us that we had families and home care agencies that would help us. Not understanding most tenants were in their 70's and above, some in their 100's may not have adult children. Perhaps they did not birth them or outlived their children, or have conflicts with them, either one stayed intoxicated, or they live across the country. Further, certainly nothing was business as usual during a pandemic.

Even before the pandemic it was difficult to acquire reliable, affordable home care services. As tenants, we soon found out how exhausting and almost impossible it was for us to do constant sorting, lifting and walking back and forth to pack boxes. Each day, I packed up the personal items that I didn't want misplaced or broken into smaller boxes, that I had to buy myself because I couldn't lift their so-called "small" boxes. Later I discovered that the company the building buys the moving boxes from, does sell a smaller size, so again why weren't they taking us into consideration, although I asked for them?

I was awake most nights mentally strategizing how to make it easier. One woman who used a walker finally told the manager that she couldn't do it. She hurt her back and her shoulder with the lifting, and it was so tiring. I had already told the moving coordinator that I couldn't have all those boxes in the way of me maneuvering my wheelchair. On rainy and snowy days, I'm unsteady on my feet and have more pain in my knees. So I'm glad someone else spoke up. When I went downstairs later to get more packing supplies from the office, the moving coordinator told me someone would come during the last few days and help me pack. I was glad because I spent four days resting in bed after also hurting my back and being so tired. Plus, I had bruises on my lower legs from bumping into boxes, that forced me to stop doing as much as I was doing.

Somehow we managed, as we wondered if the construction crew and the management of the building considered us as people. The construction crew used the two passenger elevators to move heavy new supplies, huge carts with debris, and for moving tenants' furniture in and out. They of course broke one elevator, and then the other elevator which meant that we had to wait and wait to ride the elevators. What about when we needed to get to appointments on time? They would turn off the water without notice. Some weeks they gave us letters that said that the water would be turned off a couple of days that week, supposedly so we could prepare, however the water was off all day each day that week. We'd get up early in the morning and there's no water. What about older people with incontinence challenges? It also meant we couldn't do laundry. At the meeting last year, they told us that we were going to get a new laundry room. There were only two washers working, with construction workers going through the laundry room, miserable anyway with the outside door open, blowing in cold air on us. In the fall, they took the remaining washers and dryers, having us to go two block away to the laundry mat in the winter months before the new machines came. COVID supply chain shortages was to blame.

And then they want to fine us if our apartments aren't clean on move out day? Who would have the energy by then after packing, and the stress of our routines and sanity being interrupted, with the constant sound of drilling and hammering?

Meanwhile, I made it my goal to give away or throw away as much as possible, by for every two boxes I packed I would discard almost one box full. I've collected a lot over time of course, but also because I use a wheelchair when I go outside, I got in the habit of preparing for rainy or snowy weather. Starting in October, each time I went to the grocery store I would buy double my usual amount. At back-to-school sales I bought enough paper, composition books, pencils, pens, erasers for the year. Not being able to be at the campus library in the wintertime, because paratransit vans would drive me from one end of Chicago to the other taking sometimes three hours instead of a half hour to get me to and from the University. As a result, I bought textbooks to read at home. This included other books for research papers. I really should've taken out stock in Amazon over ten years ago!

There were positives, as packing built my stamina and muscle strength with lifting, walking back and forth across the room, and from room to room to box similar items together. It felt like I was on my feet constantly. Better than an hour's workout at the gym! My apartment is now cleaner than it's been in a decade, as I dust shelves and sweep out corners. Seems silly since the construction crew will tear out the carpets, cabinets, and closets but dust was making me sneeze even with an air filter.

All of the sorting, discarding and finishing old projects is symbolic of my finishing and being done with the past. With a mixture of initial overwhelm, waves of panic, loss and grief then relief, I somehow felt safe enough, after all these decades to be able to empty out. Letting go, releasing what is no longer me. Moving on with my new, yet unknown me. Ochosi certainly didn't make it an easy transition! Perhaps it would have felt better, if I had gotten rid of the clutter, but not had to empty out my insides. Or known previously what I was physically and mentally capable of.

Chapter 12: Spiritual Transformation

Ochosi has certainly kept me returning again and again to making spiritual transformation a priority, in spite of my other plans. Although I spent many years in college, in my home life there were always crises that required faith and inner changes to get through: my near death experience occurred during my first year of nursing school, I divorced soon after graduation. African spirituality came into my life a couple of years before moving to Chicago to go to an art school that became a bridge for me studying abroad in Zimbabwe.

Returning to the United States very ill, I became physically disabled spending ten years recovering while going through menopause and an emotional long dark night of the soul. Very grateful when I discovered the Church of the Spirit and mediumship during my first year of the doctoral clinical psychology program.

Family and friends say that they are proud of me for all my academic accomplishments and degrees. However, there were plenty of times that I've cried and asked God, "Why did you give me a registered nurse degree and only let me work as a nurse for a few years? Then have to return from Zimbabwe with a debilitating illness that didn't let me use my bachelor's degree. The

Great Recession of 2008 began two years before I graduated with my master's degree in counseling. It wasn't just me who wasn't getting hired. When I talk to my schoolmates no matter what kind of counseling specialty — community, school, family or rehabilitation counseling they had to take on other unrelated jobs. The COVID-19 shutdown sidelined me for a year. At my age, I could almost give up. Why not just retire early and live on Social Security benefits? The corporate system makes sure that you're never done with "education." In Illinois, at least a year of a postdoctoral clinical psychology fellowship with supervised employment is required before you can apply to take the licensure exam, the EPPP (Exam for Professional Practice in Psychology).

But why? Why? Why? Why? I studied and worked hard, paid my own tuition throughout community college, then irrationally accrued student loans on top of student loans for a bachelors and two graduate degrees. What was the purpose?

Ochosi gave and took, gave and took. It took me years to get through my thick head, what letting go of attachments meant. The COVID pandemic crisis released the rest of my fears and attachments to people, places and things. I did not know this was a requirement for reaching my goal of getting to know what it's like to "just be." This journey "to just be" that started out 30 years ago.

Now, I no longer cry over not using my academic degrees. I've since realized that my college education helped me and others who have crossed my path or have come along for portions of my journey. The anatomy, physiology, microbiology, medical terminology, and pharmacology knowledge helped me survive life-threatening illnesses when doctors didn't have a clue what to do with me. I learned more after nursing school than during nursing school. Fascinated by psychiatric nursing courses, wanting to learn more about human behavior, I saw back in the 80's that most people wouldn't be in the hospital so frequently if their social needs in their homes and communities were addressed. Traveling abroad opened my heart to valuing people, and my eyes to see there are many perspectives and ways to live. Otherwise, I was previously stuck in thinking there is only one way, and being the best at that.

Ochosi teaches us to have balance between self and the world. This certainly taught me the hard way not to go to extremes in life. Being a strict vegan, with no salt or processed sugar in my cupboards for ten years, followed by ten years recovering from the resulting disabilities was my most challenging lesson to learn. Yet those ten years both took me down into the dark night of the soul, and raised me up at the same time.

Each of the Zimbabwean traditional healers told me their stories of how they became gravely ill, almost dying, bedridden some with paralysis requiring others to nurse them back to health. One of the traditional healers told me she temporarily had psychosis. However, at that time I was focused on gathering information for my research thesis assignment about the Zimbabwe healthcare system. They told me their stories more than once, but I wasn't thinking it could happen to me. After all, I had already almost died in 1982 returning to Earth with psychic abilities.

I completely forgot about a magazine at the Healing Earth Resources bookstore before I went to Zimbabwe. It was closing time, so the clerk was turning off the lights while talking to my friend Paula. I was standing by the magazine rack reading an article about Native American and other indigenous cultural beliefs that if you don't use your psychic and healing gifts and talents then you could become very ill or even die. The clerk hurried us out the store and gave the magazine to me for free.

When I returned to the United States, from Zimbabwe, I was only focused on survival and coping emotionally. I did vaguely remember a traditional healer who said he had discovered an herbal cure for AIDS. Would I please help him promote his herbal remedy in the United States? Was the decline in my health a punishment for totally forgetting his request? Unemployed and homeless in the city that was still new to me, I didn't have connection to people to network with, to tell them of his discovery. The friends I had prior to going abroad didn't understand my need for physical, mental, and psychic readjustment.

The true wounded healer heals one's self and then others. First, I had to heal myself physically, as doctors told me there is no treatment in Western modern medicine for degenerative neurological diseases. Second, I had to find ways to heal emotionally and socially. It seems that I also had to go through all these Ochosi trials and tribulations in order to prepare me to understand what my future clients have gone through.

Chapter 13: Career Path

Remember my second Metu Neter card career reading back in 1994? Tehuti tu tchaas /Tehuti tem maat. Tehuti represents a teacher, expert, spiritual counselor. At that time, I was new to African spirituality and didn't know what Tehuti meant except that I was to use the oracles and intuition for guidance.

I try to regularly consult the oracles. Have to be honest here, my bad, because sometimes I do get busy and am already in a situation or relationship, and only remember to consult when I start to have trouble.

Plus, since I'm usually blessed with abundance, then I get lazy and overconfident.

For my careers, including choice of clinical training sites, I do regularly consult the oracles. Soon after graduation in 2020, I did oracle readings concerning where I should do my postdoctoral fellowship. No matter what location I inquired, the guidance was for me to nurture myself first. Guidance from the, <u>Soul Lesson and Soul Purpose Oracle Cards</u>, and the I Ching readings were for me to rest, to work on my own faults, with the possibility of being misunderstood because of cultural differences, and it was not the time to start anything new. Ever busy between resting, during these two years I enjoyed being able to participate in community events, express my creativity through writing this book, making African American dolls and culturally appropriate miniatures for sandtray therapy. It was great to be able to finish projects I started years ago, easing my guilt for having accumulated all those supplies. And to not have to rush.

Of course, I wondered were there problems with my health that I wasn't aware of, and how to improve my health. So I consulted, <u>The Medical I Ching: Oracle of the Healer Within</u>, and received hexagram 52 Keeping Still, lines 1 and 2 into hexagram 26 the Taming Power of the Great:

There could be diseases from chronic stress and serious accumulations of toxins. Fair prognosis when get prompt treatment. Keeping still refers more to inner stillness and calm than being physically still.

I was recovering from repeated trauma and challenges that everyone else was also having since 2019, so I did have some mild depression and anxiety that caused me to doubt myself. Physically, painful leg and foot spasms with ankle swelling kept me awake at night. I certainly didn't want the lower legs paralysis to return. With the COVID pandemic extending past a year, I knew rest and self-care was the best way to prevent illness, so I obeyed. In the meantime, I quietly prepared for when the time was right for me to return to being out in the world.

Later, I did get a few days of COVID symptoms of severe headache, sinus infection, mild pneumonia, cough and mild fever mentioned in the Medical I Ching interpretation of hexagrams 52 and 26. Gradually I had to acknowledge other reasons why heaven instructed me to take not one year, but almost two years to rest. My physical health stayed strong as I had the luxury of drinking enough water, regular sleep, healthy meals and bowel movements.

However, I'd have waves and waves of uncomfortable memories of losses and regrets that I hadn't realized didn't have much to do with my childhood, or young adult years that I wrote about in my first book. It was mostly from the trauma I suffered in graduate school. Some of this trauma and grief is not unique to me. If you think about practicums and internships where we go to different cities, have supervisors, colleagues and clients that we establish relationships within a year. And then move on to the next location for a year. During my internship I was going to five different locations, each on a different day of the week with four different focuses at a private school, medical clinic, community mental health center and a mosque. Starting relationships and projects with others and never getting to finish it, for reasons beyond my control. The COVID pandemic shutdowns abruptly closed all of these locations in March 2020 without us ever having an opportunity to say goodbye. Same with the university I attended for six years that abruptly closed exactly a year prior in March 2019. Add this onto my previous losses and it really added up, taking a toll on mind and body. I needed this time to grieve and to get my sense of self back.

Out into the World Again

After a while with the COVID closures, I began missing interacting with people and being useful. So, I was pleasantly surprised in January 2022 to receive favorable guidance and insight into the effects and benefits of doing my postdoctoral training at EMAGES with Dr. Hattie Wash:

Metu Neter cards: Tehuti tu tchaas/Maat tu tchaas, Sacred Path Card: Sacred Space/Respect, and I Ching: Hexagram 15 Modesty

Metu Neter cards: Tehuti tu tchaas/ Maat tu tchaas means this could be a place where I could experience a contented, joyful sense of well-being and successful time, as long as I consult and follow a sage and the oracle's advice along with my intuitive wisdom.

I later discovered, when I started my postdoctoral training at EMAGES in April 2022, I would indeed be following a sage. Dr. Hattie Wash is full of wisdom and I'm continuously amazed at her truly intuitive guidance. Tehuti is an expert, a teacher and after forty years of experience Dr. Wash is certainly an expert! She is also an example of a long-term pioneer, compassionate leader, and she encourages us to also persevere in moving forward with new ways to help our people. It was definitely a Maat situation as I would not initially receive a full stipend, because most African American community mental health clinics lack funds and clients don't have insurance. I told her that was okay with me because I was there to be of service to her and the community. Her wisdom and training is more precious.

Sacred Path Card: Sacred Space/Respect. This card is a reminder about acknowledging mine and other's personal space. I do this by standing in the doorway to rooms or offices to ask permission before interrupting their thoughts or tasks before entering. It is also about respecting my own self and not neglecting my own personal needs, such as rest, nourishment and sleep while providing for other people. Along with hexagram 15, it again reminds me to respect other people's cultures, beliefs and life choices. I listen and learn from clients' daily struggles, yet creative ways to survive emotionally and socially.

I Ching: Hexagram 15 Modesty. The need to be humble and modest by being on the same social level as the average person. In this situation I too have low income like my clients, but my education allows me advantages that other people might not have, especially those from inner city areas. Again hexagram 15 reminds us to be balanced by not going to extremes. What's interesting about the guidance from the book, <u>I Ching Praxis</u>, is reference to credentials: Line 1: could succeed without showing off one's credentials; line 2: use your reputation and credentials to serve others; line 3: it's possible to earn credentials by completing your program or project; line 4: humble yourself while doing your very best; line 5: may be criticized by others regarding your credentials but what you do shows your abilities and strengths; and Line 6: may only be influential within your small community although you have well known credentials and wealth.

Since I received hexagram 15 straight up, with no lines stressed, is it possible that it really doesn't matter whether I get licensed or not? The EPPP psychologist licensure exam theories questions are outdated, with confusing wording that makes it more of an extensive vocabulary test, instead of for treatment of clients. And as far as the importance of learning and memorizing research studies results, most grandmothers will tell you, "I could've told you that!" African Americans and other multicultural people tend to fail the state exams because the questions are abstract and as we are relational people, we usually try to imagine stories as to how the information may apply to our clients before choosing our answers. Reflecting on the advice from hexagram 15 as it unfolds, I'm seeing how every line regarding credentials applies depending on what perspective and position you are in, or looking at.

On a practical level, emotionally it was frustrating trying to balance graduating with a doctoral degree in clinical psychology, as Dr. Mateen, but now learning a lot of new information and techniques specific to African American clients that wasn't taught in the curriculum at universities. How do I be humble and open to being taught, yet still be able to contribute? With so much to learn, I did at times doubt myself. The stress of the pressure to prove myself, that I didn't really want to ever have to do again, even among other African Americans. I had had enough of that in predominantly white institutions, plus often being considered dumb because I used a wheelchair.

The all African American staff at EMAGES is generous, caring but uses an honest and direct approach probably from years of counseling men. Being authentic is what I've prayed to manifest within myself and with others. Determined to not be at any agency so focused on theories, rules and policies that we couldn't be ourselves. Although I'm grateful to be in this loving, accepting environment I still had to get used to allowing myself be vulnerable again. To be able to keep my vows to be my authentic self no matter what. Hoping that the staff would want me just as I am, I gradually let go of my worries as I decided to take each day as an unexpected new day, eager to learn.

This meant not worrying about being there, in a postdoctoral fellowship position or credentials, as much as being able to learn enough to stay on afterwards and continue to help men and their families. However, as

I've previously done okay with passing exams, my credentials are needed for the success of the community mental health center, because state accreditation requires that it have licensed staff. Yet it creates barriers for African Americans to become licensed. It is a vicious cycle as we are required to have licensed staff in order to train and supervise other African American psychologists to become licensed psychologists.

I'm grateful to be trained during my postdoctoral fellowship by Dr. Hattie Wash using the philosophy and recommendations in her book, <u>Culturally Specific Treatment: A Model for The Treatment of African-American Clients</u>. Her counseling and therapy interventions are designed to acknowledge all areas of an individual's life. She explained this as four main relationship areas: biological effects on the physical body, social interpersonal, spiritual, and political/economic including the effects of racism. African-centered worldview is relational, "I am because we are." Individual talk therapy that we were taught in universities, doesn't make sense when there are multiple societal influences beyond an individual's control. Neither does family therapy make sense, based on old white middle class values of a "nuclear family" in the suburbs where the husband works, and the wife stays home. African families were extended families with several generations living and cooperating together in the neighborhood community. Dr.

Wash incorporates group therapy to help clients learn to receive and give support, to communicate, appropriately express feelings, gain a positive sense of self, respect others, and follow through on goals. Thus preparing us to restore healthy families and communities. One of my passions, as you may have noticed from reading this book and my previous book, is helping to develop ways to reestablish healthy communities.

Chapter 14: Another Tough Assignment

My postdoctoral fellowship trained me how to counsel mostly men for life stressors, substance abuse, sex offender treatment, and reentry back into society after prison or during probation and parole. This requires compassionate listening and understanding as I hear life experiences from men's perspectives. Initially it was hard to listen and not be triggered by a lot of emotions. Amazingly I didn't have flashbacks. Perhaps this is because I've already done my own hard healing work over the past few years.

But still! Counseling mostly with men was not initially one of my career plans, although I know families and the world can't be healthy and whole without men participating in intergenerational healing. Being immersed in Muslim culture for my internship wasn't on my radar either. That tough assignment came from my mother in spirit. This tough assignment of counseling men is probably from my father also in spirit, because I've asked my father to help his sons and their sons as they have repeated his same mistakes. It's not only my father's fault, it's how most men in the United States were taught to believe and behave, regardless of the dire consequences of their actions.

Families without fathers is repeated generation after generation. Fathers required to work excessive long hours away from home. Or stay away from home because of the shame of not being allowed to work. Disrespected at school, on the job, in the streets and at the mall, angry, frustrated, with a sense of hopelessness looking for a way out. America supplies the booze, drugs, pornography, video games and movies promoting excessive sex and violence as normal. A selected few get sent away to prison. Those with money go free back into society, and business as usual continues. People poor and rich are sucked into the fantasy of the highlife. Men's energy and money is more focused on winning in the sports arena then making the world a better place. Even when fathers are home, sports games may take priority over the home. Teaching boys to communicate in coded sports' abbreviations but not communication skills for loving friend, family, and community relationships.

Why was I given all these difficult assignments? Well, being in the Heru Khuti clan, why not? Heru Khuti energy is true justice, which means providing rehabilitation more than simply severe punishments. Sure, I have what it takes to yell and insult like a drill sergeant. However, Heru Khuti upholds the natural laws of Maat. On the Maat card, you'll see she holds the balance scale, but she is not blindfolded. The ability to do the right thing comes from inside each person. However, we must show people that they can have a peaceful, calm loving heart by providing safe, healthy families and communities. Instead of constantly showing us the opposite by surrounding us in the workplace, schools and media with lawlessness, greed, indifference, and violence. Our whole country, and the world needs rehabilitation and therapy!

A tough task, but we have to start somewhere. I'm grateful for the opportunity to join with others in their efforts for moving forward our human evolution. Being in the Heru Khuti and Snake clans means that I can take being bitten, attacked repeatedly, yet get up and keep going promoting truth. Sekert energy gives me the foresight, perseverance and ability to manifest towards long-term goals even if it takes decades or centuries.

This assignment from heaven also helps heal me. It takes me closer to the last aspect of my Het Heru destiny, sexuality. Even though I was sixty-six years old, the group therapy sessions with the men initially had me frequently horny and thinking about sex, like I've never felt before. What am I to do with this? Is this the way men feel, miserably physically aroused so much that they have to do something with it in order to get relief? I am an empath, meaning I feel people's emotional and physical pain, but I wasn't expecting to have to cope with this intense hot sexual energy down there, in order to understand my clients' dilemmas!

For years, men tell me, "I love your smile." "I love your voice." "Can I get a hug?" "Your Spanish is sexy." Some profess their love for me.

When men give me a compliment, I compliment them too. It's not flirting, it's my way of decreasing the gender bias. Men can be allowed to look good, have feelings, and to be authentic too.

What they feel is my peace, calm and genuineness. My Het Heru Oshun is still there with smooth facial skin, natural red lips, a slim body, subtle curves, that make me look younger than my age. Perhaps I am a little too thin, as I slide into elder age busier than before, walking more, my weight in the same range between 128 and 132 pounds, same as it's been for decades. Tell, tell aging signs as skin on my neck and arms and pants sag, and my body hair grays. Oshun is what people experience as I bring harmony and creativity to the therapy groups, helping to synchronize the co-facilitator counselor's and clients' ideas and needs. Showing everyone real love and concern.

I could laugh, giggle, play, and sing more but I'd hold back. Automatically conditioned to fear my realness will be misinterpreted. Perhaps I could try wearing the Muslim woman's burqa and niqab to cover my face, hide my smile. And not open my mouth. No conversations, not even about the weather? I don't want the men fighting over me. There shouldn't be anything to fight over because I treat everyone the same. Most people who have had near death experiences share of the unconditional love they received. Their friends and family may get a little jealous because we've been socially conditioned to be possessive and loyal to a few.

Reading the book, <u>Boys and Sex: Young Man on Hook Ups, Love, Porn, Consent, and Navigating the New Masculinity,</u> helped me understand that men's perspective and limited sexuality hasn't changed much since I was a young woman. Fear of true intimacy continues, as lies and stereotypes are circulated in locker rooms, on smartphones, and the internet instead of real sex education. This promotion of idealized sex generates billions of dollars, therefore companies don't care how it destroys families and people's lives.

Hopefully we can now restore the beauty of true sensuality, sexuality and love. When we feel satisfied and whole inside and nurtured we also feel the sensual energy in the genital area. A creative project or achievement, a home cooked meal. The nurturing closeness of a mother who cares. Curious why men have fantasies of bigger, and bigger breasts, yet, cite indecent exposure when mothers breastfeed babies in public. This closeness and connection of being supported, understood, heard, valued and appreciated can be provided by anyone — not just mothers.

Recently, a coworker gave me tickets to the Black Ensemble Theater play, "A Taste of Soul." The sensually enticing music, voices, dancing, bare legs and cleavage temporarily taking us back in time to memories, in trance to the 70's and 80's. All this is Osun energetic creativity, with the sparkly costumes and colorful stage props, along with mouth watering soul food recipe stories. Gradually I allowed in the pleasurable, fun, fun, fun! Sensually, I could have taken in more. Natural and free. Free to be innocently me and you.

Chapter 15: Applying Accumulated Wisdom to How I Provide Psychotherapy

IChing hexagram 33 Retreat. There is return after retreating, when the time is right. Here again I was returning to my career after having had to retreat and change directions several times. This time I am returning as an expert myself, with decades of acquired wisdom and formal training. Fulfilling my second Metu Neter card career reading Tehuti tu tchaas/Tehuti tem maat in 1994, now changed to Tehuti tu tchaas/ Maat tu tchaas in 2022.

I provide spiritually integrated psychotherapy for those who are interested. Meaning, for example, if a client mentions that faith helps them cope through prayer and gospel music, then we may sing gospel songs together and explore how the lyrics pertain to their life. Others may be already working on personal growth and health but are now challenged with crises that either test their faith, or renew faith with spiritual mystical experiences or miracles. Some people are astonished to learn there is an explanation for their and loved one's behavior, and glad to have their natural talents and intuition validated.

For clients with very complicated situations when I'm not sure how to proceed, I consult with my supervisor, as well as the I Ching and Sacred Path Cards at home. When I recently did this, I was amazed that the oracles accurately described the client, her situation and actually gave me similar advice as my supervisor! The use of divination is essential in African and indigenous healing practices. I don't tell clients I occasionally use divination, I just follow the guidance. However, for best results it helps to have the client, family and community's belief and participation.

Intergenerational Healing

Ancestral healing is not only for you but also your parents and their parents and grandparents. I've noticed that as I've done my personal healing my siblings have also changed and healed without going to therapy. Ancient indigenous cultures used multiple methods, some similar to how Dr. Brian Weiss recently accidentally discovered past life regression. We are collectively, globally healing as the internet and books allow us to communicate and share experiences. The truth shall set us free. Ancestral healing, well known in indigenous cultures, can now be taken to a higher level.

Much more than setting a plate at the table, talking to and remembering our ancestors. What if your core issue is that you are your grandmother who came back as you, and you are carrying her pain and fears? The psychiatrist prescribes sedatives, antidepressants, and antipsychotics medications, then perhaps in desperation gives electric shock treatments. Yet, your symptoms are still not improving. There are many people in this situation who seek relief for emotional pain and are given pills instead of getting to the real source of their pain. People need community and spiritual support, not more "newer" and newer psychiatric medications advertised on television to try since the other antidepressants didn't work. Nor tired family and friends happy for you to "Go take a chill pill."

A majority of physicians and mental health professionals weren't trained to know the difference between clinical depression versus spiritual depression. Spiritual depression as described in the book, <u>Sacred Contracts</u>, is when you feel empty inside, disconnected from everything, feel abandoned, without feeling divine love, caring and a purpose for living. Another description of spiritual depression is a "desert period," from the book, <u>Soul Perfection</u>, with an overwhelming feeling of being absolutely alone, afraid and although there are other people around it's hard to believe that anyone loves you. Or to have faith while you are tested by frequent obstacles.

Everyone will go through one or more of these long desolate periods in life. We've heard somewhat, about midlife crisis and menopause. Other cultures teach that everyone experiences major shifts that occur near puberty, at age thirty, and again near age sixty. To prepare for these common life transitions, indigenous cultures have rites of passages, initiations, and mentorships. In the United States, we expect people to stay the same throughout their lives and only celebrate transitional events with symbolic one-day parties and feasts. After that you're left on your own, to sink or swim.

There used to be convents and monasteries for young people seriously interested in a spiritual life and undergoing mystical experiences, where they were guided and protected. Now each person is scared to go through emotional and spiritual transformations on their own. People need community and spiritual support during these times.

More and more people are surviving near death experiences and other spiritual experiences with few places to go for aftercare guidance. Not knowing of natural ways, desperately wanting to replicate mystical states and connection they try out the latest street drug to temporarily obtain visions and ecstatic highs. Or turn to addictions to numb or to temporarily feel better, which could lead to unintentional criminal behavior.

The world's future is uncertain and frightening for younger generations who grew up with more media exposure to chaos, disasters and climate change. Young and old, we are all consciously or unconsciously seeking understanding and better lives, often wondering what is the purpose of bothering to keep living? True healing is integrating the ways and wisdom of our ancestors to restore whole, balanced, healthy, supportive communities by getting to know and valuing each individual's destiny and personality, as well as the community's purpose and contribution to the world.

Chapter 16: Work on What Has Been Spoiled

September 30, 2021. It was kind of late to be doing a birth chart at 65 years old. However, I noticed that my previous IChing birth chart time, done in 2008, was off by 30 minutes. The interpretation didn't make sense to me, as my other adult destiny readings usually did, about my life history.

"Hexagram 18 Work on What Has Been Spoiled/Decay. Working on what has been spoiled has supreme success and order comes into the world. It furthers one to cross the great water (meaning take on the challenges and risks to go beyond usual routine). The image of decay. Thus the superior one stirs up the people and strengthens their spirit." (Wilhelm & Baynes, 1950).

For further understanding, I consulted the book, <u>The Astrology of I Ching</u>. My life task would be, and has been, correcting the mistakes and habits of my parents that I've inherited. All of us healing and letting go of the old, so that we can bring in the new. Not understanding this earlier, has meant being depressed over not having children and a full career like my siblings. I am the only one of my mother's children that doesn't have children. Nor have I owned a home nor retired from one job with benefits. Instead, I was free to have the time, money, and education to pursue therapy to focus on healing myself. In so doing, I saw my close siblings also heal and change without going to therapy. Hopefully, we are making a dent in breaking the family cycle of abuse, to neither be the victim nor the perpetrator.

Hexagram 18 Work on What Has Been Spoiled extends beyond family to include communities and governments. As you may have read in my previous memoirs, I have worked on what has been spoiled for most of my adult life, without consciously knowing these tasks were part of my destiny.

A friend requested I pull a Jewish Kabalah, <u>72 Names of God</u> card, after I told him about the ninety-nine names of Allah book and cards. Repeating the specified prayer on one of the cards, and carrying the card with you opens the way to safety, contentment and more. Did I have room to add another similar culture's beliefs? Curiosity and dedication won out. I asked the question, 'What do I need to help me through this stage of transition, and best be able to help?' It should be no surprise that it is 61 Water: Vav Mem Bet, with the meditation prayer: "With this I purify the waters of the earth and awaken the forces of healing and immortality." This card reading certainly does relate to my interest in helping others heal and to understand the continuity of life.

It seems odd to end this book here. And I was going to, but then during editing, I realized I left out the third orisha that the Candomble priestess told me ruled my head, Osaala. It took me awhile to find out that Osaala is a Spanish language intonation for Obatala. Afterwards, I did not give conscious thought to Obatala. I didn't wear white nor do any prayers or rituals for Obatala. Ashamed that I honestly forgot Obatala all these twenty years.

Tears come to my eyes as I read the attributes of Obatala, from the book, <u>Obatala: The Greatest and Oldest Divinity.</u> His attributes describe me in my older years, as I return to what I consider is a career. Gentle, quiet, calm and patient, yet is a leader with good character who serves humanity to help reform the world from chaos and distress by finding solutions to problems whenever needed. And to redeem generational curses. More tears. Sounds similar to "work on what has been spoiled." Helps others to fulfill their destinies. Orisha means destiny. May have a disability or assist those with disabilities. No alcohol and avoids red meat. Able to find peace and harmony to overcome fear and sorrow. This attracts blessings for self and others. I've been wondering how abundance comes easily to me. All of this is true.

I've shied away from being a leader, but that's what I'm called upon to do. People criticize my calm and patient style, especially since I counsel clients who had rough backgrounds. I was recently doubting my approach, thinking, well maybe I should be tougher. No, this is how I am meant to be. I'm always automatically problem-solving, even in my sleep. What does this person or another need? Each person has unique needs. You would think this would drive my head crazy. Reading this about Obatala helps me understand, instead of resist, my destiny role. A role I've been doing all along without knowing. Obatala exists in modern society. We could all strive to live the virtues of Obatala.

Conclusion

Writing this book took some unanticipated twists and turns. It started as one book and became two separate books. There were long pauses as I awaited intuitive guidance for what direction to go next. The ending was completely unexpected, as I was astonished to learn more about my hidden destiny path after all these years. Faith, trust and regularly following the oracles led me to these revelations.

Hopefully, you have a trustworthy spiritual counselor or mentor to help with interpretation of your divination, in regards to your personal growth and situation. In life we learn by doing, by experiencing, not by continuously reading or listening to lectures, or memorizing scriptures. A genuine spiritual counselor can guide you through because they've also been through what you're going through. Especially through the longer periods of intense individual and collective societal growth. The resultant peace, courage, confidence, joy, miracles, and abundance is worth the effort.

With meditation and reflection, you will connect to your own knowledge and experiences. Trust what you intuitively know and your honest observations of the world. Everyone, each person has an important piece of wisdom to share that was broken apart centuries ago, that is gradually coming together again for the whole betterment of all. My intention is to introduce you to indigenous ways that were taken away from us. So that you are no longer afraid of your own culture, nor of people who live their cultures. I showed you how I apply what I've learned to my everyday life. Now it is your turn.

With deep respect for indigenous cultures and the people who truly have the knowledge I thank them and yield to them. My prayers are for all indigenous communities globally to be recognized and respected, most importantly their culture and lands returned to them, and allowed to be restored to healthy ecological balance. Exploitation and stealing resources from people here in the United States and from other countries ceases. Amen.

In my upcoming third book, <u>Getting to Know Yourself and Others: Multicultural Personality Studies</u>, to better assist you, I go more in depth, giving personality descriptions beyond my own experiences.

As you can see, I could have delved even deeper into learning and living any specific one of these ways of divination knowledge. It would be helpful, for other dedicated people to follow my lead and write books about how the use of divination changed and enhanced their lives.

All the best.

Books and Articles

I purposely did not write this book in a scholarly way, with huge academic words, book quotes and citations. This is because we all have this knowledge and information within us. Books are just one way to share and communicate with each other. I believe there really is no such thing as an expert, it is simply one person sharing their opinion and experiences. The so-called expert may have done the research and statistics to find how many other people might agree. And they had the money and the time to get published. But life is always changing.

Meaning what was true two weeks ago, may not be true today. And the authors may live in a completely different situation than yours, and therefore the advice may make no sense for your current life situation. Books are a way to have a long-distance conversation, often with a stranger. But inside us is enough commonalities, so that we don't feel alone. Here is a list of books whose authors think similar to my experiences, and some who don't.

Boys and Sex: Young Man on Hook Ups, Love, Porn, Consent, and Navigating the New Masculinity. By Peggy Orenstein. Harper Collins Publishers.

Culturally Specific Treatment: A Model for the Treatment of African-American Clients. By Hattie Wash, Psy. D. (2018). Lulu.

Decisions Decisions: Getting Answers to Life's Challenges: Volume 1 Getting Started. By Haneefa Mateen (2023).

Decisions Decisions: Getting Answers to Life's Challenges: Volume 2 Returning. By Haneefa Mateen (2023).

Decisions Decisions: Getting Answers to Life's Challenges: Volume 3 Sidelined. By Haneefa Mateen (2023).

Holistic Tarot: An Integrative Approach to Using Tarot for Personal Growth. By Benebell Wen (2015). Berkeley, CA: North Atlantic Books.

I Ching: A New Interpretation for Modern Times. By Sam Reifler (1974).

I Ching: The Tao of Drumming. By Michael Drake. (1991). Talking Drum Publications. (paperback). Random House Publishing Group. (e-book).

I Ching Praxis: Forty Years of Practical Insights into the I Ching. By Ra Un Nefer Amen (2014). Khamit Media Trans Visions, Inc.

Isese Spiritual Workbook: The Ancient Wisdom of the Ifa Orisa Tradition. By Ayele Kumari, PhD. (2020). Ori Institute.

Light Emerging: The Journey of Personal Healing. By Barbara Ann Brennan. (1993). Bantam Books.

Metu Neter Cards. By Ra Un Nefer Amen (1990). New York, Khamit Corporation.

Metu Neter Vol. 1: The Great Oracle of Tehuti and the Egyptian System of Spiritual Cultivation. By Ra Un Nefer Amen (1990). New York, Khamit Corporation.

Mother's Love from Beyond: A Healing Journey of Grief and Loss: A Memoir. By Haneefa Mateen. (2021).

Obatala: The Greatest and Oldest Divinity. By Olayinka Babatunde Ogunsina Adewuyi (2013). River Water Books.

Ochosi: Ifa and the Spirit of the Tracker. By Awo Fa'lokun Fatunmbi (1992). Original Publications.

Past Life Oracle Cards. By Doreen Virtue and Brian Weiss, M.D. (2014). Hay House, Inc.

Phoenix Rising: No-Eyes' Vision of the Changes to Come. By Mary Summer Rain. (1987, 2011). Hampton Roads Publishing Company. BookNook.biz (e-book).

Physicians of the Heart: A Sufi View of the Ninety-Names of Allah. By Wali Ali Meyer, Bilal Hyde, Faisal Muqaddam, Shabda Khan. (2011).

Sacred Contracts: Awakening Your Divine Potential. By Caroline Myss. (2002, 2003). New York: Random House Company.

Sacred Path Cards: The Discovery of Self through Native Teachings. By Jamie Sams (1990). New York: HarperCollins Publishers.

Sacred Path Workbook: New Teachings and Tools to Illuminate Your Personal Journey. By Jamie Sams (1991). New York: HarperCollins Publishers.

Soul Lessons and Soul Purpose Oracle Cards: The Most Direct Path of Spiritual

Peace and Personal Fulfillment. By Sonia Choquette. Hay House, Inc.

Soul's Perfection: Journey of the Soul series, Book 2. Sylvia Browne. (2000). Hay House.

Spirit Song: The Introduction of No-Eyes. By Mary Summer Rain. (1985, 1993). Hampton Roads Publishing Company.

The Astrology of I Ching. (1976, 1993). By W. K. Chu and W. A. Sherrill. Penguin Books.

The I Ching or Book of Changes. By Richard Wilhelm and Cary Baynes. (1950). Princeton University Press.

The Illustrated I Ching Workbook. R. L. Wing. (1987). Aquarian Press.

The Medical I Ching: Oracle of the Healer Within. By Miki Shima. (1992, 2011). Blue Poppy Press.

The 99 Beautiful Names of Allah. Physicians of the Heart: Wazifa Card Set. By Shabda Khan, Faisal Muqaddam, and Bilal Hyde. (2022). Mandala Publishing.

The 72 Names of God: Meditation Deck. By Yehuda Berg (2004). Kabbalah Publishing.

Women of Sufism: A Hidden Treasure: Writings and Stories of Mystics Poets, Scholars and Saints. Selected and introduced by Camille Adams Helminski. Shambhala Publications.

Wrapping Authority: Women Islamic Leaders in a Sufi Movement in

Dakar, Senegal. By Joseph Hill. (2018). University of Toronto Press.

Author's Bio

Haneefa Mateen has a wealth of life experiences and knowledge from exploring healing methods for mind, body and soul. A natural teacher, healer, and artist she shares more of her wisdom. Her books are accessible, easy on the eyes, available in large print format.

She has an associate's degree in registered nursing, bachelor's in International Studies, master's in Rehabilitation Counseling, and a doctorate in Clinical Psychology. She currently does spiritually integrated therapy and healing, and is active in

African American community cultural events.

www.ingramcontent.com/pod-product-compliance
Lightning Source LLC
Chambersburg PA
CBHW020522080526
44583CB00013B/702